To Lucy & Simon
Best wishes always
may all of your dreams ~~~~
Your friend
Charlie DeLeo

Charlie DeLeo:

Keeper of the flame
2-9-11

Keeper

of The

Flame

WILLIAM C. ARMSTRONG

see me on
You-Tube

Copyright © 2006 by Armstrong Associates
2514 S. Gardenia Place
Broken Arrow, Oklahoma 74012
Phone: 918-254-1300

Keeper of The Flame
by William C. Armstrong

Printed in the United States of America

ISBN 1-59781-929-8

www.xulonpress.com

CONTENTS

CONTINUED

CONTENTS

CONTINUED

* See 8-page center fold showing
   dramatic photos of Charlie in
   action at the Statue of Liberty!

*F*oreword

Charlie is well known worldwide. His unique role as "Keeper of the Flame" at the Statue of Liberty has been picked up by the media and spread abroad over three decades.

In 1990 he was photographed atop the Flame, waving the Stars and Stripes (see cover). *PARADE* ran the photo on the front cover of their magazine, going to 40 million readers.

From there *Reader's Digest* let the whole world know about Charlie. Overnight, he became a folk hero, featured in over 100 newspapers, radio and TV interviews, and articles in several books.

The book, *Charlie DeLeo: Keeper of the Flame*, is a true story of an amazing young man, brought up in poverty, with little education, a Vietnam "Purple Heart" veteran, who followed his childhood dream of becoming "Keeper of the Flame" at the world's greatest monument dedicated to Liberty and Justice for All.

The impact of his overcoming faith speaks loud and clear to all ages, especially young people who need to know what it means to be a giver and not a taker, to know the Lord, and to know how to follow Him all the days of your life.

I can assure you, the more you read and know about Charlie, you're going to really love the guy.

William C. Armstrong, author

ONE

Tenement Dwellers

Within walking distance from Battery Park at the southern tip of Manhattan, lies a multi-cultural section, the Lower East Side, known for such tourist favorites as "Little Italy" and "Chinatown." In the early 1900s, many immigrants settled in low-rent tenement housing in this area of New York City.

The neighborhood became a mixture of Italian, Irish, Hispanic, Asian and Jewish people. With little money, facing barriers of language and culture shock, they learned to survive. Breadwinners took on menial tasks to make ends meet, while the youth chose to join those of the same national origin and form gangs to gain their identity.

For some the will to survive became the will to succeed. Among these was a Russian Jew who immigrated to the U.S. from Russia at age 4 with his family in 1902. Israel Baline grew up, selling newspapers and singing on street corners, and became a singing waiter in Chinatown.

This humble little man attended school only two years, with no formal music education. He went on to become known as Irving Berlin, America's great songwriter and composer of *God Bless America,White Christ-*

mas, and many of the top songs of the 20th Century.

It was in this environment that Charles DeLeo was born on March 18, 1948, to parents Vito and Molly DeLeo. His mother was previously married to a man who was stabbed to death in a bar, leaving her with two babies. A young widow at age 19, with two children, Molly married Vito DeLeo. They had two children, Charles and a daughter, Christine.

"My mother's side was Greek, and my father's side was Sicilian," says Charlie. "My father had a falling out with his parents and never once took us to see my Italian grandparents. But I did know my mom's relatives. They came from Lemnos, an island off of Greece."

Growing up on the Lower East Side, Charlie loved to hear the family reminisce about how his grandfather came to America, went through Ellis Island, and got a job in a bakery in the Bronx. He'd wake up at three o'clock in the morning and get ready to make the long trip to work where he took on the jobs of two men to make enough money to later send for his wife back in Lemnos.

"I especially remember a funny story of around the time of United States' entry into World War I. Grandpa went to sign up for the draft. He knew very little English, only Greek.

"When he joined other men in line, an officer announced, 'Okay, those who want to enlist in the U.S. Army, raise your hands!' Poor Grandpa thought he was in the line with those signing up for the draft, so he raised his hands with the rest of them. Before he knew it, he had enlisted in the army!

"But it was a blessing in disguise. As soon as he

enlisted, he took the oath of allegiance to the United States of America and became an American citizen. Finally, when he got discharged, he sent for Grandma. Since they were already married, she automatically became a citizen. So it worked out pretty good."

To Charlie, his grandmother was like a saint. His mother was the joy of his life. But he never could relate to his father. When other kids would brag about their dad being a good role model and serving in the war, Charlie would make up stories about his father to hide the truth. "I wanted a father I could really be proud of. I didn't know much about him. He was very mysterious. He never told us kids about his childhood, never would introduce us to his parents.

"I learned later that the reason he never served in the armed services was that, at age 17, he had committed a felony. He was involved in a robbery with some guys. I guess he needed the money. He served a few years in prison for that crime, which barred him from the military."

The DeLeos were poor, living in and out of welfare, barely making it, as were others in the low-income neighborhood.

"My mother had a tough life, but she was always loving, making the most of what little she had. For breakfast she'd give us children a slice of bread each and tell us, 'Dip it into your coffee. It will fill you up.' We ate a lot of potatoes and macaroni, couldn't afford meat. At least we had something nourishing to eat.

"She was always concerned with making my life happy in spite of the poverty. She made sure I had my Saturday night bath and put on a clean shirt for church on Sunday."

As a boy, Charlie didn't exactly look forward to

going to the Greek Orthodox service at Easter. "I still remember the smell of the candles, the long flowing robes of the bearded priests with their ornate headgear, holding high their sceptres, as the procession moved slowly and majestically down the central aisle of the cathedral-like sanctuary.

"I was able to endure in the midst of all the pomp and ceremony, and to some extent I was even intrigued by the theatrics of it all. But I fidgeted and squirmed my way through the endless two-hour rituals, all proclaimed in the Greek language, not one bit of which I knew, except the word, 'Christos,' meaning 'Christ.'"

Charlie could tolerate the Catholic services which his family regularly attended at that time. They were mostly in English, with some Latin phrases chanted at the altar. Growing up, Charlie became infatuated with the high-pitched solos of "*Ave Maria*" (Hail Mary) and "*Panis Angelicus*" (Holy Bread) sung at Mass.

"But it was really my mother who drew me close to the Lord. Her enduring faith and genuine maternal love are still with me to this day — very much so! In spite of my father's harshness and aloofness, I found meaning in life through my precious mother.

"With six of us crowded into a tenement, barely surviving on welfare and surrounded by poverty, in a densely populated area known for gang warfare, drugs and crime, I still look at that time in my life as the 'happy days.' "

Charlie had a lot of friends. His first childhood buddy was Joseph Caruso, known as "Jo Jo," whose parents both worked. Jo Jo had a new bike, roller skates and a TV which Charlie didn't have until he was older.

Later on, he found a friend in Pat Masconi, a wild

guy, nicknamed "Patty The Ape," a bully who beat up on kids in the neighborhood. "There was a time when we had a fight, and even though he whipped me, he respected me after that and we became good friends.

"Living next door to us was a wonderful Puerto Rican family with four boys. Their mother was quite a lady. Another good friend was 'Perez.' His mother was Jewish and father was Puerto Rican."

Charlie, like most kids growing up in New York City, enjoyed the unique kind of neighborhood street sports — stickball, punchball, "Ring-a-leavio", "Johnny on the Pony", and "Red Devil". And for thrills, Charlie and his pals would venture below the Manhattan Bridge to an underpass where the train tunnels were.

"We'd walk on the third rail and when we heard a subway train coming, we'd climb into a crawl space until the train passed by. It was dangerous but we were all game. We were tough kids!

"Over the years, we made hundreds of trips down there on the tracks. When the sandhogs were building new tunnels, we'd go down there at night with a box of sparklers. When one sparkler went out, we'd light one after another to see our way in the dark.

"Now and then, the sandhogs worked with a 60-foot crane in the daytime. In the evenings, Patty the Ape and I climbed to the top of the crane and then slid down the rubber hose from the top of the crane to the ground! It was fun!"

Another adventure was climbing from one apartment roof to another and, in the winter, throwing snowballs on people below. One time, their target was a cop who raced up the stairs after them. They escaped by climbing over to the next roof and vanishing out of sight!

"I have a whole lot of great memories of my youth growing up on the Lower East Side! My greatest experience was knowing Miss Alfa Briggs, an African-American, a very distinguished Christian lady, who was supervisor over the Park House, a recreational area in our neighborhood.

"She really loved all of us kids. We were like her family. She didn't care if we were black, white, red or yellow; we were her boys and she took care of us. If we fell or got bruised or cut, she'd give us first aid. She made us honorary Park workers and gave us 'New York City Park' pins which we wore with pride.

"I loved the summers, when we'd go swimming in the Park pool. I enjoyed every minute!

"I looked forward to our Christmas Party at the Park House. Miss Briggs would get merchants in the area to help fund the party. A grocer, named Gary, was chubby and played the role of Santa, and a woman put a pillow under her costume and played Mrs. Santa. I loved when they opened the Christmas stocking filled with gifts for all of us!"

Though Charlie was never in a gang, they protected him, especially the Puerto Ricans in the Forsythe Street Boys. In the neighborhood, the toughest gangs were the Knight Dragons who had four chapters — the Golden Dragons, Young Dragons, Imperial Dragons, and themselves.

"When the gangs began to rumble with each other or with the Italian gangs in Little Italy or the gangs from Chinatown, it was serious business. In one encounter, a couple of members from each gang were shooting zip guns at each other, when a 16-year-old girl passing by was shot and killed on the spot! I never saw so many police cars converge on the Park so quickly. It was sad."

Yes, New York's Lower East Side was a place where the war between good and evil was fought moment by moment. But, out of that battle emerged champions — overcomers like Irving Berlin and Charlie DeLeo who were destined to make their mark in the midst of conflict.

TWO

The Patriot

Charlie couldn't afford a bicycle. Now and then, he had enough change from cashing in pop bottles to rent one for 30 cents an hour. When he turned eight, he fell in love with a snazzy red bike with whitewall tires on sale at Andy's Bike Shop for $8.

At that time, his father was working, so his Mom was able to scrape up the money for Charlie to own his first bicycle!

"One day my friend Patty and I rode our bikes to Battery Park where I got my first glimpse of the Statue of Liberty out in the harbor. My eyes were glued on Lady Liberty. She fascinated me, and I kept saying over and over, 'I love that Lady!'

"At Battery Park I was in awe as I stood before eight marble tablets with the names of servicemen and service-women from around that area of Manhattan, Brooklyn and Staten Island, who had given their lives during World War II. Above the memorial was the figure of a majestic eagle with wings spread, the symbol of America. At that young age, a spirit of pride and patriotism welled up inside me!"

The next year, Charlie visited the Statue of Liberty for the first time when the teacher took his fourth grade class on a field trip to the world famous landmark.

"I was absolutely mesmerized with the Statue. She was more than a statue or monument. I saw her as a beautiful lady. Next to my mom, she was my favorite gal of all!

"The girls screamed with a mixture of fear and delight as we began climbing the 168 steps up the spiral staircase to the crown of Lady Liberty. I thought it was a blast. I couldn't wait to get up there. Through the windows of the crown, I spotted the tablet in her left hand and, looking up, I focused on the torch held high in her right hand."

To Charlie that torch was special. He was told it represented the freedom that the Lady stood for. Today, looking back on that trip, he realizes, "For the first time, the good Lord was introducing me to my calling to Lady Liberty on that school trip in 1957 when I was in the fourth grade at P.S. 42 in lower Manhattan."

Charlie and Patty liked to ride their bikes across the Brooklyn Bridge, one of the first suspension bridges ever built. Dedicated in 1883, it was hailed as the "eighth wonder of the world," the tallest free-standing structure in the United States.

Its stone towers stood 270 feet above sea level, a record that lasted only three years until October 28, 1886, when the Statue of Liberty was dedicated, towering 305 feet above the New York harbor, from sea level to the torch.

The main reason Charlie liked to cross this bridge, rather than Manhattan Bridge or Williamsburgh Bridge, was that he could enjoy a good view of the Statue of

Liberty.

"Little did I know that her shadow hung over me, that God had a great plan for my life in the future with Lady Liberty, and it would be above and beyond my wildest dreams!"

During his teen years, Charlie became a movie buff. The Loews Delancey theater was first class. It cost 50 cents to see a couple of movies. But the Windsor theater, known as "The Dump," was the favorite. It cost only 29 cents to see three movies, plus a free bag of popcorn, a comic book, and 10 cartoons!

"It wasn't clean and had an odor about it. But I can remember I saw some of my greatest features there — 'Earth vs The Flying Saucers', 'The Incredible Shrinking Man', 'Godzilla', 'When the Worlds Collide' and many other thrillers!

"Another movie I loved was 'The Land of the Pharaohs', also 'Helen of Troy', and of course, the great Biblical movies I watched at Loews Delancey — 'The Ten Commandments', 'King of Kings', 'Quo Vadis' and 'The Robe'."

Those were the carefree days. Then came Nov. 22, 1963. Charlie was 15 years old, in the tenth grade at Central Commercial High School, sitting in the afternoon class at a calculating machine, when an elderly teacher entered the room to make an announcement.

"Boys and girls," he said, "I want you to stop what you're doing, grab your coats, and get ready to leave." His countenance was grim as he paused, then said simply, "Our President Kennedy has been shot, and are are to stand by."

The students sat with their coats in their laps. Fifteen minutes later, the teacher returned. This time he was in tears, barely able to make the announcement,"Boys and girls, I want you to know President Kennedy has just been . . . assassinated. I want you to . . . file out quietly."

That afternoon, Manhattan traffic seemed to be moving slowly. No sounds of the honking of horns, not even by cab drivers. People were walking with their heads down. Men, as well as women, were weeping openly in the streets, on the buses, and on the subways. It was a blow to all Americans, especially to Charlie DeLeo.

"Politically, I was very conservative," he mused. "Had I been old enough, I would have voted for Richard Nixon. But I liked President Kennedy because he was young, in his early 40s."

On the way home that day, Charlie made up his mind then and there, "When I am old enough, I am going into the military service to serve my country. No matter how good my grades are, I will leave school and join the armed forces."

The next two years, Charlie was enrolled in Food and Maritime Trades High School. As he got closer to his 17th birthday, he began nagging his parents about joining the military.

"I had always wanted to go into the Army Airborne. I loved the Marines, especially after seeing John Wayne as 'Sergeant Striker', and I loved the Army Airborne after watching 'The Longest Day.'

"I liked the idea of jumping out of a plane. But my parents wouldn't consent to my doing that — it was too dangerous. Since, at age 17, I needed my parents' consent, I said, 'What if I go into the Marines? They don't jump out of planes — they land on beaches.' My parents said, 'O yeah, you can do that,' and they signed the papers.

"When I told my teachers that my parents gave

their consent for me to join the Marines, they were surprised. They couldn't believe it.

"At that time, believe it or not, I had the highest average of my school career. In all six subjects, including the meat cutting course and the commercial courses, I had an 89 average and was on the honor roll.

"I was doing the best I had ever done, because I had a real interest in teachers teaching me things that I liked. I loved world history. They taught me about the ancient Greeks. I loved that because I am Greek on my mother's side. I hated art, but I still had an 89 average in that class!

"So when I told my teachers I was dropping out of high school to join the Marines, they said, 'Hey, Charlie, you're bright enough to go to college and maybe get a scholarship! Are you crazy?'

"They warned me, 'You're going to go to Vietnam and get killed! Don't do it! Stay in school!'

"I had every intention of going to Vietnam. I was a staunch conservative. I really deeply believed that Communism was as ruthless as Nazism and Fascism, and that communists were determined to take one country after another until they had conquered the earth. That's what they were all about! They would not stop until they conquered the world.

"Besides, I was determined to help any country keep its freedom and fight the Communist menace, thereby not allowing America to be encircled by countries taken over by Communism.

"Being very patriotic, I was determined to do that. When I was a kid, one of my big heroes was Davey Crockett. In 1955, I watched Walt Disney's film about 'Davey Crockett, King of the Wild Frontier' with Fess Parker. The 'Lone Ranger' was a a hero to me. Roy Rogers was also a hero. He and his wife Dale Evans were Christians, and used to have a kids ranch. I was hoping some day I'd be one of those kids chosen.

"My favorite TV show of all was 'Annie Oakley,' starring Gail Davis. She was so pretty in her pigtails. I loved her and had my first boyhood crush on her."

Charlie was very patriotic. He was devastated when the Russians launched Sputnik in 1957, and even more so when they orbited the first man in space in 1961.

"I was scared they were going to get to the moon before us, and would establish military bases there, and have nuclear missiles aimed at America from the moon! For a few years they were beating us but, once we got the momentum going, it really was no contest from there on.

"I was fiercely proud of my country and its achievements. I also knew that America was free to give aid to a lot of Third World countries.

"No country has been more benevolent than America. No nation protected other countries of the earth as we did in World War II. We literally saved the free world from the Nazi/Fascist menace that could have taken off and wreaked global havoc."

THREE

"A Few Good Men"

Charlie, now 17, with his parents' consent, and having notified his teachers of his determination to quit school and join the Marines, in a spirit of "gung ho" headed straight for the Marine recruitment center near City Hall.

To his dismay, he took the test and failed it. But that wasn't about to stop this overcoming patriot. The recruiting officer suggested he buy a book that would help him pass the test. Charlie bought the book, read it, and was able to pass the test.

"I was told to report at Whitehall Street for my medical exam. Two days after I took the exam, I was asked to see the recruiter who told me, 'Charlie, you passed everything but the eye exam. I'm sorry, we can't accept you into the Marines.'

"I was devastated. 'Why?', I asked. He said, 'Because, Charlie, your vision is not sharp enough. Even with glasses you might not be able to pass the rifle range. You have to fire at targets from a distance of 500 yards.

You would never be able to see the target.'

"I was broken-hearted, felt like my world had hit bottom."

Another recruiter saw the determination in the young 17-year-old and approached him, "Charlie, I'm going to try to get you a waiver from Washington. Then, if you get to boot camp, you can get glasses that might help you see the targets. We'll see what happens."

As at many crossroads Charlie had faced in his young life, he had that "knowing" inside that his Lord and Savior Jesus Christ was moving on his behalf. And the broad grin that brightened his face showed it!

The waiver came through on April 12, 1965, marking the beginning of Charles DeLeo's four-year enlistment in the Marines!

Charlie describes his introduction into the U.S. Marines in vivid detail:

"I was sworn in by a Marine Corps officer at the induction center in Manhattan along with 60 other recruits. We took the oaths and the next day boarded a plane at LaGuardia airport for Charleston, South Carolina.

"From there, I got on a special bus, with 50 other recruits, heading for the Marine Corps depot at Parris Island. We were all singing and joking, eating candy and cracking jokes until the bus driver announced,'We are now approaching the Marine Corps depot at Parris Island.'

"The Marine sentry checked us out at the main gate and the bus went on until it came to some old wood-framed barracks, painted black and white. Waiting for us was a man about 6'2" tall, wearing a Smokey the Bear hat, and looking real mean.

"The door of the bus opened; the Marine instructor jumped aboard and yelled out in a voice that would have made John Wayne tremble, 'Now, you slimey maggots, you've got five seconds from the first to the last man to get out of this bus. And when I say "Move", you move!' *(I am cutting out the cuss words!)*

"Then he yelled 'MOVE!' in a voice that would have made Arnold Schwarzenegger shudder! And we just about trampled one another, all 50 of us, trying to get off that bus! We knew we were in for something, and it was something we would not be particularly happy about for a few weeks.

"That night we slept in the staging barracks, and all I could think of was those DI's (drill instructors) really giving us a hard time. When they sounded taps, lights out, I just lay there, staring at the ceiling.

"I said, 'Dear Lord, this morning I was still a civilian and even before we all took the oath of allegiance to the USA, that Marine Corps captain told us, *'If you don't think you are physically or mentally able to go through boot camp, you can walk out right now before you take the oath, and nothing will be said about you. But, once you take the oath, you belong to the U.S. Marine Corps for four years, for better or for worse.'*

"I was saying to myself, *'Boy, I should have walked out of here!'* We were all young, 17, 18, 19. We didn't realize it was the job of these instructors to get the 'civilian' out of us, toughen us up, and train us as U.S. Marines.

"The way they were screaming at us and treating us like animals, we thought those instructors were all a bunch of maniacs!

"The next day we were assigned to Platoon 322 under Sgt. Lee Robert Ward and three junior drill instructors. Sgt. Ward was husky, tough, and mean — a veteran of 17 years in the Marine Corps. When he looked at us, we just about melted!

"The first few days were difficult. First thing on the agenda, they shaved our heads, making us look like a bunch of mobsters! After they issued our utility uniforms, and we donned our fatigues, we looked more like prisoners!"

From there, they were marched to classes to find out which talents the Marine Corps could use. One might be a cook, a clerk, or a truck driver, but each was expected to be a rifleman first and foremost. That meant one could be pulled out of his job at any time, and be placed on the frontlines as a rifleman.

"Since I had worked for a butcher and was trained in meat cutting at a food training school as a civilian, I was classified as a meat cutter. After all these tests, the regular training started. I remember my first encounter in the mess hall and how the DI marched us to chow that first day He barked at us, 'Now you've got five minutes from the first man to the last man to get in and out of this mess hall.'

"Those cooks put the food on our metal trays; we sat erect and ate in strict military routine, trying to gobble down as much food as we could, because the training was very physical and demanding, and it was a long time between meals!"

The next thing, each recruit was issued an M14 rifle and taught everything about it, including how to break it down and put it together, even blindfolded so that in a combat situation, at night, he'd be able to clean it or unjam it.

"We were told how our landing craft might be 100 yards from the beach, and we'd have to swim that far or at least dog paddle. They taught us how to float, how to blow air into our utility jackets so we could stay afloat, and how to keep our weapons dry as possible.

"At first we were the laughing stock, but as the weeks went by, we started to look pretty good in our drilling. They taught us how to spit shine our shoes and boots, how to pack a sea bag and be ready for standard inspections of our living quarters and bunks."

Running the obstacle course and confidence course came next. Some obstacles were 70 to 80 feet high, along with a slide for life and a cable crossing.

Sgt.Ward kept insisting on one thing, that the most important goal for a Marine recruit, next to graduation, was to qualify with his rifle at the rifle range. He and the other sergeants relentlessly hammered this into the recruits. It would be the greatest test of all for Charlie. That was what the recruiting officer back in Manhattan had warned him about.

"Before the rifle range, they introduced us to something I never want to go through again. It was called the gas chamber. They took us to a place a few miles from Parris Island. It looked like a wooden lodge house with a potbellied stove inside where they cooked the tear gas.

"A few of us went in at a time. The instructor had his gas mask on, and showed us how to put ours on. Then, he started putting pellets in that stove and the smoke started to rise.

"Everything was beautiful until he said, 'When I tell you recruits to take your gas masks off, start reciting the words to the Marine Corps hymn!'

"Sure enough, we did it, but I only got through *'from the halls of Montezuma'* when I started to cough and jump up and down. Man, I was suffocating!! That was the most horrible feeling! My lungs and throat began to burn, with tears coming out of my eyes and snot coming out of my nostrils!

"Finally, we all came running out, the sorriest looking bunch of guys you'd ever want to see!

"They told us, 'Don't touch your skin —you'll burn yourself! When you run outside, put your hands high in the air and start running for all you're worth and let the air take the sting out!'

"I don't ever want to go through something like that again. Once is enough!"

Next, the Big event — the rifle range!

A primary marksman instructor (PMI) showed the recruits how to get into their different slings — the kneeling position, the squatting position, the prone position, and the standing freehand position. Each couple of recruits had a rifle coach helping them get their windage while zeroing in on their target.

"I was scared that, even with my glasses on, I wouldn't be able to see the target on the 500-yard line. I needed to get a 35 out of 50. If I didn't get at least a 35, I would not qualify. And for the overall test, I needed a score of 190 to qualify!

"Fortunately for me, I had a very inspirational instructor who knew I would have a problem with a distance of 500 yards. He kept pounding it into me, 'You can qualify! You can do it!'

"He told us, 'If any of you shoot 210 out of a 250 top score, I will take you to dinner and buy you a steak!' He gave me a lot of confidence. But all I cared about was a 190 — I wanted to qualify!

"We had four days of non-qualification tryouts. On two of the four days I qualified over 190, but two of the days I went under 190. The day before going into qualification, I shot a 180! I figured there was no way I was going to make it!

"But the drill instructors that night announced, 'If any of you did not qualify today, I want you to go to the chapel.' And I knew what he meant — he wanted us to pray to the Lord that He would give us the grace to qualify with our weapons.

"I prayed hard, *'Lord, if I don't make the rifle range, even if I graduate from boot camp, I'll never consider myself a Marine. Please, just give me the strength and the eyesight that I can shoot a 190. Because, Father, today I only shot a 25 from that 500-yard line. Please, help me!*

" *'I know You are not for war and anything like that, and You never meant for Your children to kill one another. But I love my country and I've got to defend my country. And I know that is honorable with You because You were always with the children of Israel in their wars. You've got to get me through this time!'* "

Sure enough, on qualification day, God answered Charlie's prayer. He shot his best from the 500-yard line which he had dreaded — 45 out of 50, 20 points higher than the day before!

"By the grace of God and His goodness, I qualified with a 209.

"The rifle range was behind us. We were now in the fifth and final phase of our recruit training. From there it was all downhill. We were guaranteed to graduate!

"Our platoon marched to chow that day, waving a red streamer which meant we had the highest average on the rifle range. I was on cloud nine!"

Another proud moment for Charlie was at graduation. Out of the 70 recruits in a platoon, the top seven recruits made Private First Class (PFC) and received a stripe for their uniform. Also, the highest marksman was honored as "the highest standing recruit," and received a gift of free dress blues.

"Sgt. Ward was calling the names of the PFC's when all of a sudden, I heard him call my name and announce, 'Out of all the recruits in our platoon, no one has tried harder than Charlie DeLeo. Charlie, you step up here, for you are now going to be PFC DeLeo!'

"For the longest time I hadn't even thought I would graduate from boot camp. I didn't think I'd pass the rifle range. But I always tried. And here I was chosen as a PFC, one of the honored seven. An incredible moment!"

From Parris Island, Charlie and his fellow graduates boarded buses for Camp Lejeune in North Carolina for eight weeks of advance training and one week of mess duty. But, like Charlie says, "That was a 'piece of cake' compared to the pressures of boot camp at Parris Island."

"Finally, they sent us home on our first furlough. I can remember how proud I was to be a Marine. Everywhere I went, I wore my dress uniform, and I got some nice looks from a lot of pretty young ladies, even some pretty older ladies.

"I was always shy with the ladies and wouldn't dare try to get friendly with one. But they sure gave me fair notice in that Marine uniform!

"I'd be strutting down Fifth Avenue and along Broadway, and every time I saw a flag flying from a building, I saluted. It turned out there were so many flags, I thought I better let one salute take care of all of them!

"My mom and dad were so proud of me, and also my grandmother and grandfather. It was so great being a Marine!"

FOUR

Enroute to Vietnam

After his furlough in the fall of 1965, Charlie was assigned as a meat cutter back at Parris Island. His job was to help prepare meat for eleven mess halls that fed thousands of recruits coming through boot camp.

It involved a lot of hard work, cutting meat up into hindquarters and forequarters, and then breaking it down for chops, roasts, steaks and hamburgers.

"I delivered the meat on a big tractor trailer with a civilian driver, making sure each mess hall had its allotted quotas. The truck driver was a 60-year-old African-American, a charming gentleman named Candy. Very wise and always pleasant, he reminded me of Miss Briggs, the park supervisor who was an influence on my life growing up in Manhattan's Lower East Side."

On weekends, Charlie would put in for a weekend pass and try hitching a ride to nearby Savannah, 42 miles south of the base.

"I remember a ride with three Marines. The driver was from Mississippi, the other from Tennessee, and one from New York State.

"After two days of taking in tourist attractions, on Sunday night we headed back to the base at Parris Island. All of a sudden the rear tire went flat. The driver had a jack but no lug wrench. With no way to change the tire, and time running out, we were heading for AWOL."

"Out of nowhere, a car pulled up alongside us. The driver, a middle aged African-American man, saw the problem, reached for his lug wrench, helped us jack the car up and changed the tire.

"When we offered him money for helping us, he answered, "Absolutely not!" He got in the car, wished us well, and with a smile on his face, drove off.

"Thanks to that living sermon from that wonderful black man, we made it to our base on time. I thank God for that man, for he really lived the Gospel. I saw Christ living in him."

At work Charlie met Ralph Tambasco, a fellow Marine and meat cutter from Amsterdam, New York, of Italian heritage like Charlie. They became close friends and their friendship grew as they shared the same desire to serve their country in Vietnam.

On Sundays Charlie liked to run the confidence course at Parris Island. He'd climb the ladder on a pole up to the tower where three steel cables were hung. From there, using only his arms and hands, he shinnied all the way down the cable — 200 feet to the bottom!

"I'd repeat that exercise three or four times. It made my arms really strong. Also, I'd run and do calisthenics. My main reason for all this was to be in shape for Vietnam.

"After a while Ralphie and I grew tired of Parris Island, because, being personnel, we had to set a high standard for the recruits in boot camp. That meant there were a lot of inspections."

So both men put in for overseas duty and were sent to the Marine barracks on the island of Guam, part of the Marianas in the South Pacific. Charlie was assigned to Company A and Ralph to Delta Company.

"I was doing guard duty at the main gate where I had to wear white gloves and carry a 45 holster. We could carry a magazine with bullets but were not allowed to load unless our sentry post was in danger.

"I had five hours of guard duty in the day and three hours at night. The daytime duty was a 'piece of cake', but the three hours at night, I had to fight wanting to sleep, especially when I was assigned to the wharf where cargo ships would dock and unload."

On Guam the U.S. Naval Station and Marine barracks were on one end of the island, and the Anderson Air Force base at the other end. Naval personnel numbered about 10,000 sailors and 200 Marines. At the Air Force base, there were another 12,000 airmen.

B52s were taking off from Anderson Air Base on Guam to Vietnam and Okinawa to bomb enemy targets. Cargo ships docked in daytime and, on one side, unloaded their bombs, including the 500 pounders, 1,000 and 2,000 pounders — and on the other side, the bomb fins.

"One particular night I had the 1:00 to 4:00 a.m. shift. I was totally exhausted. When I relieved the guy at 12:59, I was ready to sleep. But I said to myself, '*Charlie, you've got to stay awake - walk around, walk around!*'

"The crews on the ships were all sleeping. I was the only one supposed to be walking around, guarding hundreds of these bombs and tail fins, making sure that no one tampered with them. It was a real lonely and scary job because there were hardly any lights.

"I was fighting the need to sleep — on and off, and on and off, until finally, at 2:30 in the morning, I took my M14 rifle and crawled under a flatbed truck loaded with the bomb fins. I figured I'd sleep for only a few minutes. I must have gone out like a light!

"The next thing I knew, a light woke me up. It was a Navy shore patrolman who shined his spotlight on me, sleeping with a weapon! My eyes flew open, and I thought, *'This is it! Court martial! Brig time! Definitely a bad conduct or undesirable discharge!* Nothing is worse than being caught sleeping on guard duty, guarding bombs going to Vietnam!

"Fortunately, I knew the shore patrol sailor, a wonderful black man, a nice looking young guy. He stood there laughing. 'You know, Charlie,' he said, 'when I hit you with that light, I had already let you sleep for ten minutes. And then I just had to shine the light on you to see your reaction. I knew you'd pop up scared!'

"He added, 'Look, get up and walk around because your sergeant on guard could show up any time and you could get into a lot of trouble!'

"If I had been caught by the officer of the day, I would have been immediately arrested and probably received a pretty severe court martial. But this wonderful young black man saved my hide. I thank God for him!"

Charlie was friends with a few Marines. But the others were always dating attractive young ladies, daughters of government personnel on Guam. Charlie was too shy to ask a girl for a date, so he became involved in fitness.

"I liked to walk alone, especially at 10 or 11 at night when all the stars were out. They seemed so much brighter than they were back in Manhattan.

"A lot of times I'd stop and pray. I had always felt close to God and that He was watching over me. But, at 18 years of age, I realized a strange thing was happening in my life — I found pleasure in being alone, even though I felt the pain of loneliness.

"I've always believed God put me on this earth, and that He would one day match me up with a Christian woman. All I cared about was that she would be faithful and dedicated, true to the Lord and true to me, and I'd be true to my Lord and true to her.

"I wanted someone with a kind of inner beauty, who would be a good wife and a loving soul.

"I didn't know how to have fun with a woman— partying, drinking or dancing. I'd rather she and I enjoy watching a sunset or sunrise together, than to take her to any dance, concert, or movie. I'd just like to take a girl walking by the seashore, or looking at the stars from a hill- top, or walking through a field of flowers or trees.

"I have a favorite song that expresses how I feel:

I believe for every drop of rain that falls,
    a flower grows.
I believe that somewhere in the darkest night,
    a candle glows.
I believe for everyone who goes astray,
    Someone will come to show the way.
I believe . . . I believe.

I believe, above the storm, the smallest prayer
    will stll be heard.
I believe that Someone in the great somewhere
    hears every word.
Every time I hear a newborn baby cry, or

touch a leaf, or see the sky.
Then, I know why . . . I believe.

"I believe in the simple things of life, the free gifts of God and I believe in Jesus Christ, His Son, as my Savior."

After serving several months on Guam, Charlie yearned for the opportunity to be a part of the action in Vietnam.

"Now and then I'd go to the mess hall, and there would be Marines transferring from Vietnam with orders to serve guard duty on Guam. I'd look at their Vietnam campaign ribbons, Purple Heart ribbons and Silver Star medals, and wonder when the opportunity would come for my time on the frontlines.

"I wanted to go to Vietnam, not so much to get those medals, but to do my part in helping contain the spread of Communism, and to keep the South Vietnamese free from the aggressors. I felt that very strongly!

"One day I was working with weights in the gym, when all of a sudden a sergeant came in from personnel and announced, 'I need a volunteer for Vietnam.' Guess whose hand shot up first — mine!

"The next day I was in his office, filling out papers to transfer to Vietnam. The first thing I told the sergeant was, 'My only service is as a meat cutter, but I want to go into the infantry and fight. I want to be a grunt. It has nothing to do with food service.' "

He said, "I can't do anything for you now. Your orders are to fly out of Anderson Air Force Base to Okinawa for two weeks — one week of mess duty and one week of staging, getting ready to go to Vietnam. Then, when you get to Da Nang, you present your orders and tell them you want to join the rifle company."

" 'Okay, that sounds good to me.'"

The next morning Charlie and two other Marine volunteers from Guam boarded a KC145 for a seven- hour flight to Okinawa where they spent a week of mess duty and a week of staging, getting ready to go to Vietnam. Charlie's friend Ralphie stayed behind on guard duty on Guam.

"Finally . . . tomorrow I'll be in Vietnam!" thought Charlie, his face aglow with his dream about to come true!

FIVE

"...for all is vanity."

Ecclesiastes 3:19

"On April 16, 1967, at 1 p.m, we were flying over Vietnam, about to land at DaNang Air Base.

"Looking at the countryside below, my first thought was, *'Hey, there's a war going on down there. I'm wondering if I'm in a plane for the last time in my life! I might not make it out of this place!'*

"Actually, at first gaze, the foliage and vegetation looked beautiful, and so did the country, surrounded by the South China Sea.

"We landed and went direct to the air terminal to present our orders to the Marine lieutenant. I told him, 'Sir, I want to volunteer for the infantry. I have a meat cutter's MOS, but I'm here to fight.'

"He said, 'I don't think you've got enough time in a rifle company where we can place you with a rifle company right away. You don't have the experience, other than boot camp and advance infantry training. We're going to send you to Phu Bai, 80 miles north of Da Nang, where you'll be part of the Fourth Logistics Command. We're sending you to Fourth Logistics Support Group Alpha, where you'll present your orders to the mess sergeant.'

" 'The mess sergeant?,' I said in shock. 'That's a cook. I don't want to be a cook!' "

He said, "Well, the only openings we can give you are a mess duty, a bakery, or a motor transport. I think the jobs are filled for motor transport, and to begin with, you don't have a government license. So what do you want, the mess hall or the bakery?'

"I said, 'I'll take the mess hall. But, sir, how soon can I request a transfer to the infantry?' He said, 'You've got to be in the country 90 days before you can do that.' "

Charlie reported to the mess sergeant at the mess hall at Phu Bai. He was then introduced to the chief cook and told him, "Look, I don't know beans about cooking. I never went to school for that."

"Well, you'll learn," was his answer. "The other cooks will teach you."

Charlie soon learned that being a cook, especially in a combat area, meant you worked long hours and very hard, beginning at 3 in the morning and ending late in the afternoon. Furthermore, it was hot in Vietnam, especially working with the portable field ovens.

"I hated being a cook. In my eyes, I was a warrior, a Marine rifleman. There was no way I wanted to say if I came back from Vietnam, 'Hey, I was a cook!'

"But I'll tell you, there's nothing dishonorable about any job you do in life or in a combat situation. If you do it faithfully and with dedication, you have served your country with honor.

"So I labored hard, worked my tail off, and sure enough, when 90 days came up, I requested a transfer to the rifle company.

"At that time, my friend Ralphie had volunteered to transfer from Guam to Vietnam, and he tracked me down at the mess hall. He was assigned to the infantry, a rifle company in the First Battalion, Fourth Marines.

"I was envious of him. I wanted to know how he did it. But he told me, 'Dee, when I was in Company D on Guam, I hated it there. But then, when I got to Vietnam, I was on a convoy and we were ambushed. I was so scared, I was wishing I was back on Guam.' "

It wasn't long before Charlie had a similar kind of experience. He had been in Vietnam only three months and had already experienced a couple of minor mortar attacks. But then, on August 10, 1967, right after midnight, came the Big one!

"We were all in our hooches. If you're in a support logistics area, you live in hooches, made out of two by fours with plywood walls and corrugated steel roofs,with sandbags on top to keep the steel from blowing off.

"All of a sudden, we heard 'thump, thump, thump . . . mortars exploding in our compound, and Marines yelling, 'INCOMING! INCOMING! INCOMING!',with sirens going off all over the area!

"Everybody in our hooch (there were ten of us) beat me out. On my way out, I saw Sullivan, one of our cooks, lying there drunk. He had really tied one on at the enlisted men's club that evening, and had conked out during the mortar attack!

"I punched him in the leg as hard as I could, shouting at him, 'Get out of here. . . it's INCOMING . . .INCOMING!!! He got up and beat me out the door!

"I knew something was wrong. Right after they started yelling 'INCOMING', I remembered feeling a sharp pain in the upper left part of my leg, not far from the groin area. I realized I got hit with a piece of shrapnel, but I first had to get out of there and into a bunker!

"These bunkers were not very safe. There was one layer of sandbags on the top and two layers around the sides. If we had taken a hit from an 88 mortar, we would have all been gone! The attack was over in five minutes. We found out later three Marines were killed and 52 wounded!

"I didn't consider my hit a big wound. I didn't even think it needed any attention, maybe a couple of bandaids and iodine. But my buddies insisted I go to the field hospital.

"The hospital was like a regular hooch but a little larger, with no room for cots. Wounded Marines lay on the plywood deck floor, some of them bloody messes!

"I told the corpsman, 'Hey, these guys need attention. I'll wait outside until you're ready for me.' After two hours, the corpsman told me, 'I'm going to give you an injection to ward off any infection.' He cleaned the wound and applied ointment and a large bandaid, and told me to see him in a couple of days.

"I knew one of the three Marines who were killed. I had been talking to him a few days before in the enlisted men's club. He was a 19-year-old like me, from Macon, Georgia, working for motor transport.

"Here I was, in Vietnam only a few months, and I had seen six of my brother Marines lying in their own blood. This was the war, and it was real, deadly . . . killing!

"I realize you can get killed even in the rear support companies. The chances are, by all means, far greater in the infantry but still, you're in a war zone, and mortars kill just like bullets!"

"One of the cooks had a dog named Boober, a beautiful female pooch that I helped feed. We had an outdoor makeshift theater with a wooden platform, a white sheet for a screen and a projector. As we watched a movie, I remember Boober was trying to sleep on my lap, and I was getting a little annoyed because I couldn't concentrate on the movie.

"I kept brushing her away. After the movie ended, I went back to the barracks to find Boober had given birth to a litter of cute little puppies.

"An hour later, the cook who took care of her, came running into our quarters, hysterical! He had found Boober in the shower room, lying in a pool of blood. Her throat had been cut! She was suffering, with no hope of surviving. The sergeant of the guard took out his 45 and placed it to her head.

"Some of the Marines looked away. I kept looking at Boober as the sergeant fired the bullet. Her head swung upward and her jaws opened wide. She laid her head down and died.

"Another Marine and I carried her body to the back of the compound, dug a little grave and buried poor Boober, wrapped in a blanket."

Later on, two of her pups were found with their heads decapitated. Everyone knew who had done it — one of the Marines, a psychopath. Nobody liked the guy. They were scared of him because he really was crazy, in need of a medical discharge!

Some of the Marines, including the cook that owned Boober, loaded their M14s, and went looking for the guy. If they had found him, they would have killed him that night.

"O, man's inhumanity to man and to animals —

how horrible! I'll never forget old Boober for as long as I live!"

A lot of the cooks liked to go to the enlisted men's club and booze it up. When they had the opportunity to get into one of the villages, they'd try to make out with the girls there. But not Charlie. He just wanted to work out and keep in shape.

South Vietnamese men and women were employed at the compound in Phu Bai, doing laundry, running the barber shop and other jobs like that, while the older "mamisans" worked in the mess hall, peeling vegetables, serving food and cleaning.

"One of the workers was a petite 18-year-old girl named Wu, whose face was like that of a most beautiful angel. She was a Catholic, like me, and wore a cross. She liked me and I kinda liked her.

"I was not shy with Wu like I was around other women. She would have made me a good wife — so gentle, sweet and kind. I had never met anyone like her. But I didn't want to get serious with her because I was in a war zone, to begin with, and I might not make it back to the States. Even if I did, it might have been difficult to be married to a South Vietnamese woman, surrounding her with a whole new culture in the United States.

"The last I heard, when I was back in the States, the South Vietnamese army was trying to draft her to help fill their ranks. I just pray that God protected Wu. She deserved the best husband. She was wonderful!"

Now and then, a company of infantry troops came through the chow line at the mess hall, dust-covered grunts just coming off the frontlines of battle. Charlie served them with great respect, and with a longing to join them in the war against Communism.

"Little did I know that it was the hand of God that was keeping me out of danger and saving me for something that I would understand later on."

Charlie was a frustrated warrior. One time he cut himself while shaving and when he was treated for infection, he asked the corpsman, "Can I donate blood?" The answer was, "I'm sorry, Charlie, all our blood is frozen, flown in from the States. We don't have the facilities here to take your blood."

"Hey, they won't let me fight, and now they won't even take my blood!" said Charlie in disgust. "What kind of an outfit is this?"

But, even as a cook, he'd get caught in the crossfire. One night he stayed at the Da Nang Air Base before flying out in the morning on an assignment.

"At one o'clock in the morning, we heard the sirens go off and the yells, "INCOMING!...INCOMING!... INCOMING!", emanating from the air base where bulk fuel is stored in tanks for the transports and jet flyers! We were outside, with no bunkers for covering!

"These were not mortars coming in — these were rockets, the big boys, and I was facing toward the tanks filled with bulk fuel!

"All of a sudden, a direct hit by one of the rockets and all the bulk fuel went up in one shot — a massive fireball 1,000 feet high!!! So big was the explosion it knocked me and several Marines down to the ground.

"The heat was so intense, it felt like a blowtorch going off in my face! The report came in later, 'A few Air Force guys killed in the explosion!' "

"The moment the bulk fuel tanks got hit by that rocket, it was just like something you'd see in a movie. It made you feel very close to God in an instant, that you are finite and He is infinite!"

Charlie was awarded the Purple Heart, but turned it down because he felt the wound was not big enough to merit such an honor. But his company commander told him emphatically, "You will receive it, and that's it!"

"As we stood there in formation the day they awarded the Purple Heart to 52 of us Marines, I noticed out of the corner of my eye Marines nearby were loading the body bags of the three dead Marines into metal containers to fly them back to the States.

"I thought of what Solomon said, 'Vanity, vanity — all is vanity!'"

S I X

Sandbags and Body Bags

"Seeing the body bags of the three dead Marines being loaded on the plane that day made me want to join the infantry out of vengeance. I kept trying to volunteer every chance I got.

"Finally, I was able at least to transfer from mess duty to a small utility company where our job was to repair hooches and do a lot of fixing up around the different bases.

"I remember being on a convoy that passed through Hue, the ancient Imperial Capital of South Vietnam, a beautiful, colorful city with ancient Buddhist temples that had been standing there for centuries."

The time was nearing January,1968, the beginning of the Tet offensive when the North Vietnamese and the Vietcong would be making an all-out effort to force the U.S. Marines out of I Corps in the northern part of South Vietnam, not far from the DMZ where North Vietnam began.

During the nine months that Charlie had been in

Vietnam, both sides of the conflict had enlarged their forces, and the number of casualties increased dramatically on both sides. And now, beginning with the Tet offensive, the Communist forces launched large-scale attacks against urban centers and military bases in South Vietnam.

"The next time I saw Hue," Charlie remembers, "there wasn't much left of it. It had been pretty well leveled!

"Ordinarily, serving in a logistics company, we were not allowed to have live ammunition. But, if we were going to be attacked, then we would be issued bullets. But with the Tet offensive underway, Marines, whether truck drivers or cooks, got their hands on ammunition on their own and loaded up the magazines of their M14 and M16 rifles."

At midnight, December 31st, weapons started going off everywhere! A fierce battle was raging, with heavy damage and loss of life in Hue and Khe Sanh. The longest battle of the war had begun in Khe Sanh.

Charlie's utility company was ordered to go to Khe Sanh to pick up equipment for the field hospital there — a dangerous assignment.

This was the opportunity Charlie was looking for. When he volunteered to go, his commanding officer at first refused. "Charlie, you have only 37 days until you are to be rotated back to the States."

"But, sir," said Charlie, "please let me go, if just for a little while. They've kept me out of the action and I never did get to serve on the frontlines. I really would appreciate it, sir, if you would allow me to go, even if it's just for 30 days."

He said, "Well, I'm going to let you go but I'll allow you up there only a few weeks, and then I'm going to pull you out of there."

"Thank you, sir."

"We were to fly in a C130 from DaNang to Khe Sanh where the airstrip had already been pounded relentlessly by the enemy, resulting in a large number of Marine casualties. They would drop us off there, where we were to wait for a shipment of washing machines to be coming in at a later date on another plane. Then we would deliver them to the field hospital in Khe Sanh.

"As we approached Khe Sanh, a crew member aboard informed us, 'When we land, our motors will still be turned on. The first thing we're going to do is unload some supplies. They're on skids and on tracks, ready to roll. Next, you guys, when we tell you to move, get out of here on the run! As soon as the last man is off, we're taking off!'

"Circling the airstrip, we caught a glimpse below of a chilling sight — what was left of a C130 completely demolished by enemy fire power! Nobody had anything to say. You could hear a pin drop! It was scary!

"After the supplies were wheeled off, the crewman said, 'Okay, Marines, get out!' And we filed out quickly with our backpacks, helmets and rifles. About 50 feet from us was another Marine, waving us to take cover at the nearest bunker.

"We were expecting to get hit at any moment. I was the last guy out. The C130 lifted off in safety. It was like something out of a war movie — incredible! Overhead were the Huey Cobras. That meant we were getting air cover!"

Charlie and the other five in the utility company from Phu Bai submitted their orders to the commanding officer who had been through the entire 77 days siege of constant mortar and rocket attacks at Khe Sanh.

"When I met him, he was pleasant, but I could see he was a bit nervous. The word was, through some Marines, that he had suffered a little shell shock. Looking over my orders, he mentioned, 'You know, you don't have that much time. Are you going to extend?'

"I said, 'Yes, sir. My desire is to extend to six more months and get back to Phu Bai. I want to be in an infantry company.'

"He said, 'Well, I know what you guys are here for. We'll let you know when your washing machines land on the airstrip so you can take care of that. Until then, you'll just have to be doing regular duty, helping fill in sandbags or fortifying bunkers.'"

Khe Sanh was the hottest spot in the war at that time. And yet it was really beautiful country. It reminded one of the Marines of his home state of Georgia — the green hills, red clay dirt, and top soil.

As to military quarters, gigantic pits had been dug, surrounded by layers of sandbags. Inside were trucks, jeeps, and people living in huge steel containers, with a door for access coming and going.

Inside the containers were four racks on either side, with bed mats and two chains to hold them up or down. This was home for the next 12 days for this utility company of six men.

While waiting for word of the arrival of the washing machines, they were kept busy on work details most of the day — building bunkers or fortifying them, even digging ditches with picks and shovels in red clay dirt that was like cement.

"The hardest part was that we were allowed C rations that went back to WWII and the Korean War, and no hot food - and only two meals a day! But we soon discovered a way out. Not far from where we were was an Army compound that had no shortage of C rations.

"In one little area, guarded by a chicken wire fence, they had palettes of C rations, cases of them. And theirs was the good stuff made in the 60s — like spaghetti and meat balls, and roast turkey!

"A couple of us guys said, 'Why don't we go there at night and steal the C rations? We would have all we want for the time we're here. All we need is a wire cutter.'

"One of our guys cut the fence so we could get in. We must have taken 25 cases of C rations. We ended up feasting like royalty!"

One work day Charlie came across a big pit filled with water from the rain. Marines had suspended from a tree, with branches hanging over the water, a chain and a tire for young kids to swing on over the water.

"There was this one young South Vietnamese boy, not more than 10 or 12. Man, he was having the time of his life on that tire, swinging and laughing and jumping in the water again and again!

"I looked at that boy and felt a great sadness in realizing that he could be an orphan. I thought, 'If the war doesn't go well and we don't win it, what about his family?' I felt, for the first time, a great sense of pity and compassion for him. I was really concerned about the welfare of the South Vietnamese people!"

Asking around among the Marines stationed at Khe Sahn, Charlie found out that an old friend of his, D.J. Lynch, was with a Marine battalion dug in on the hills 400 or 500 yards from the airstrip at Khe Sanh.

"D.J. was an Irishman from Staten Island, a bull of a man, a Victor McGlaglen type. If you ever got in a fight, he's the one you'd want close by you, the kind of guy that could wipe out half a dozen guys in a barroom brawl! We had been together in Company A on Guam in the Marine barracks. He was a character!"

One morning Charlie in his flight jacket with the zipper left wide open and without a helmet or weapon, went looking for D.J. If Charlie were surprised by a VC or North Vietnamese on the way, that would be the end of him. But he was determined to locate the First Marine Battalion, Ninth Marines and find D.J.

It was steep climbing up those hills. He kept passing different companies of Marine grunts that told him where that battalion was. Charlie climbed another 60 or 70 yards up to the top of a hill, and there was old D.J. and a bunch of Marines!

"They were all drinking, and they offered me a drink. I didn't want to say no. D.J. hugged me, and we talked about old times on Guam, and that Ralphie Tambasco was with First Marine Battalion 4 and was okay. He told me that he himself expected to go up on the front-lines real soon.

"His battalion had engaged the enemy on several occasions on fire fights. When I told him I was going to try to extend six more months and get into his company, his eyes got big. 'Dee, you're crazy to try to extend,' he said, leaning forward, eyeball to eyeball with his old buddy. 'You go home in one piece! I'm telling you!'

"D.J. was a good old boy. But I was determined to do what I had to do. We hugged again, and I left, heading for the airstrip at Khe Sanh, a mile away.

"On the way back I had to make my way down steep hills covered with short bushes with thick stalks sticking up. I didn't realize it then, but most of them had been sharpened by the Vietcong so that, when the enemy lost their footing, they would be impaled on one of those stakes!

"I found out the hard way, that the VCs would rather have you wounded than killed — because it takes four Marines to carry you out, which slows them down, creating an easy target.

"When I started down this hill, I was startled by a figure suddenly appearing on the scene! I looked up. It was a Marine lieutenant coming out of nowhere! He said, 'Marine, zip up that flight jacket!' I obeyed his wise command.

"Moments later, I lost my footing and was soon tumbling uncontrollably down that perilous slope! I could see a bush in front of me and realized I was headed straight for one branch in particular, sharpened as a stake!

"There was no way to move right or left. I was going to crash into it and was scared of it impaling me in the face! I kept getting closer and closer to it. Finally, I hit the sharpened, spear-like stake with a tremendous force that knocked me to the ground on my back!

"If God hadn't sent that Marine lieutenant to warn me to zip up my flight jacket, which had been wide open, I would have been stabbed right through the heart. I would have been killed instantly!

"Right then and there, I knelt down and looked up at the beautiful blue sky with white clouds, a bright sunny day. I said, 'Dear Lord, my God, I know you saved my life. No doubt about it. Thank You, Lord!'"

Still, the plucky little Marine from the Lower East Side of Manhattan was determined to extend his enlistment six months in Vietnam in order to serve in the infantry.

That night, one of the Marines from his utility company told him, "Hey, Dee, I hear they need volunteers to work in Graves Registration." Charlie jumped at the chance to be a part of the action. He knew what that meant, and his answer was, "Okay, I'll go."

"I went down there to offer my services and one of the guys working at the Graves division said to me, 'Okay, corporal, here is what you've got to do. See that body there? Take this cotton and a bucket of water, and wash the blood off that body. Then we'll bag it up.'

"It was a young Marine, with nothing on. He had been stripped. He couldn't have been more than 19 or 20, an infantry man. He had a hole in his chest that would hold a tennis ball. His left leg, from the knee down, was blown away. He had his arms folded like he was just resting. His face had a peaceful look.

"I just didn't have the stomach to wash him down and help bag him up. I didn't have the stomach to work in Graves, with the smell of death everywhere. I told that corporal, 'I can't do it. I'm heading back.' "

He said, "Okay, you don't have the stomach for it. I understand. You can go."

Charlie headed back, past the airstrip. The Huey helicopters were landing, and in them were dead Marines. Live Marines were unloading the bodies, laying them on the airstrip, some covered with blankets and some not. What was left of them was clearly visible to those passing by.

"I saw them. They were young like me. Right then and there, I had no stomach to extend my enlistment, to try to go into the infantry. Suddenly, I wanted to get out of Vietnam in the worst way.

"I felt this was a horrible war, one that we could

have won militarily very quickly had President Johnson, our commander-in-chief, wanted our military to conduct the war and win it. But I felt there was a lot of politics involved in it, and it was a no-win type battle.

"I saw it as a gigantic waste of the lives of our servicemen, our allies, and even our enemies who were suffering. All war is horrible! But this was particularly horrible because it lasted so long, with the poor South Vietnamese taken over and enslaved anyway!

"When we eventually pulled out, the Communists committed genocide, killing over a million South Vietnamese men, women and children. And maybe two to three million Cambodians were slaughtered as well. It was just a horrible situation.

"During this time at Khe Sahn, for the first time in my life I felt that maybe preserving life was a lot better than taking life. I wanted to go home. I had no more stomach to try to extend another tour of duty, get in the infantry, and get killed.

"I realized that God's mercy was heavily upon me and it was time to go. I had done the best I could, and by God's grace I was delivered. Even though I was never in the infantry, I had been through several mortar attacks and a couple of rocket attacks and had been hit with some shrapnel; it was time to go!"

Charlie found out later that the washing machines never did arrive. After 12 days he received orders from the major and began waiting for a plane to fly him back to Phu Bai, and from there, home.

One line of Army troops was waiting to fly out of Khe Sahn, and also a long line of Marines. Finally, a C130 landed and picked up some Army and some Marine personnel, including Charlie.

"I remember stopping off at Phu Bai where I had to wait one more day and night. Then I would be heading for Da Nang and then, from there, homeward bound!

"That night, would you believe it!, we got a mortar attack, and we all ran outside because those bunkers at Phu Bai were not too good for protection. When the 'all clear' was given, we went back to the hooch. Sure enough, right over where my little bunk rack was, there was a hole in the roof. The shell had gone through the roof, missing my little cot, past the plywood deck and into the dirt!

"We had to keep away from the hooch until engineers could disarm it. They found it was a dud!

"That night I praised God for again sparing my life."

After turning in his gear at Phu Bai, Charlie was flown to Da Nang and from there to Okinawa for a week's leave of going through personnel, getting ready to fly home to the States via San Francisco and finally landing at Kennedy in New York!

"When the plane took off from Da Nang, leaving Vietnam for San Francisco, I felt a great sadness and yet a sense of peace, a salvation I received from God as He spared my life in spite of my doing anything I could to endanger my life, especially volunteering for duty in Khe Sanh, the heart of the longest and fiercest battle of the Vietnam War."

Again, little did Charlie know that God was getting ready to do something so wonderful with his life, that it would be like a screen play written for a movie!

SEVEN

Destiny's Moment

Charlie had eight months left to serve in the military before he would be discharged in April, 1969. Assigned to the Marine barracks in Key West, Florida, he knew he'd get guard duty and he had had enough of that on Guam. So when there was an opening for a cook at the U.S. Naval Station, he went for it.

"The Navy required two cooks from the Marine barracks. Sure enough, the sergeant major assigned me to the mess hall, a million dollar facility where the Navy cooks treated me great.

"I learned to roast meats the Navy way, and they turned out good. I liked rooming with two Navy cooks in our own cubicle. What a difference compared to those days in Marine boot camp with 60 men living in close quarters in a crowded barracks!"

During his stay in Key West, Charlie spent his off hours helping archaeologists, who were working for the Navy, to explore one of the old Spanish forts in search of relics. They didn't find any cannons, but discovered 48 cannon balls. To Charlie, it was fascinating work.

"One time, acting on a hurricane warning, we had to board up all windows and doors at the Naval Base. The mess hall remained open 24 hours a day to feed emergency crews and provide them hot coffee. We ended up catching the tail end of the hurricane before it headed out to sea."

Charlie especially remembers Christmas 1968, the day Apollo 8 orbited the moon.

"I was enjoying a steak dinner at the enlisted men's club, with my eyes glued to the TV. Walter Cronkite was talking to those brave astronauts who were making history — Frank Borman, the commander, James Lovell, Jr. and William Anders."

The cameras showed a close-up of the lunar surface, then switched to the weightless astronauts inside the rocket orbiting the moon, and then back to the famous newscaster.

"My spirit was with those astronauts. How I wished I could be aboard with them! I sat in awe as they read from the Bible, in outer space, the first verse of Genesis:

In the beginning God created the
heavens and the earth.

"I was so inspired by that because I don't believe in evolution. I believe that everything is just too perfect out there, that a Great Intelligence is behind all creation, and not this idea of evolution which is soulless, brainless, and dead.

"God created nature and uses it as His handmaiden. It is God and Christ who created nature.

"Evolution is the face of the hopeless. It is so absolutely illogical! Just look at the human body, the function of the brain and the eyes. Why do we have emotions? Why does man have a noble spirit and, at the same time, can be so cruel?

"We are all created in God's image. He created us and gave us a free will."

Charlie was to be discharged from the U.S. Marine Corps in April, 1969. Instead, he was given an early out in January, 1969 and was flown to New York to receive his honorable discharge as a Corporal E4, with two stripes and two rows of ribbons.

Some time before he joined the Marines, when he was still at home, Charlie and his family moved from the Lower East Side in Manhattan to a larger home in Brooklyn. The house owned by his grandparents had burned down, so Charlie's family and his grandparents and uncles all decided they'd move into a two-story home and live together.

It was in a nice neighborhood in the Cypress Hills area of Brooklyn, very quiet, with nice neighbors. But Charlie missed his old neighborhood where he had grown up.

A large "Welcome Home, Charlie!" sign was taped to the front of the house at 205 Hemlock Street in Brooklyn, New York. As the handsome young Vietnam veteran stepped out of the cab in his sparkling Marine uniform, the family surrounded him with love and gratitude to God for his safe return.

His mother's cry echoed in his ear as she kissed him, repeating over and over, "Thank You, Jesus! O, thank You, Lord!" Charlie was home!

The very next day, his first priority, even before getting his discharge from the Marine Corps, was to put on his dress blues and head for the Statue of Liberty.

"I took the Circle Line ferry. On the way over I stood atop the boat in front of the captain's wheelhouse.

As we approached Lady Liberty I went below and made sure I was the first one off the boat.

"I hit the ground running, the first one to reach the Statue, and kept running all the way up the 168 stairs (the equivalent of 22 stories!) to the crown, huffing and puffing!

"The view was even more glorious than I remembered from my school days! I breathed a prayer, thanking the Lord for sparing my life in Vietnam and allowing me to experience the blessed liberty of being back home in America!"

Noticing the doorway to the ladder going up to the Torch, he was reminded of his childhood wish to someday be able to climb that ladder to the Torch. He thought, "Maybe, if I ask one of the Park rangers to have a little pity on me, he might let me go up to the Torch, seeing I am just back from Vietnam."

The ranger, when approached with the request, told Charlie, "I'm sorry. I know you've just come back from Vietnam and I respect you for all you did, but the Torch is closed. Only the superintendent can give that clearance, and he is not here today. But, if you'll leave your request and your phone number, I'll see what I can do."

" 'That's okay, thank you anyway,' I said. Then I walked around the island and looking up at the Torch, I said out loud, *'Dear God, is it possible for You to get me up in that Torch one time before I die? I'd love to be up there one time, Lord!'* "

Charlie returned home, with the stark realization that he was again a civilian, needing to find a job and establish himself in a work that would fulfill God's calling upon his life, whatever that might be.

Jobs were scarce, and Vietnam veterans were viewed on the whole as being trained for warfare but not necessarily for the work place. During the first six months, the young veteran painted his parents' entire house, applying two coats to most of the rooms. It kept him busy. Then, in 1970 his father got him to join the union. He worked off and on at a half dozen construction jobs, none of them steady, including demolition work, knocking down elevator shafts, renovating old buildings and working with bricklayers.

"I liked it because it was hard, physical work, and because I was in such good shape from being in the Marines, I was able to handle heavy construction laborers' type of work. But it wasn't steady. There was just not a lot of work available back then in the early 70's."

Charlie decided to offer his experience as a meat cutter and landed a job in a meat packing plant, Berliner and Marx. "I started work at 2:00 in the morning at the Washington Street market on the west side of Manhattan. I didn't like leaving home at 12:30 midnight, to go to work.

"They had me loading trucks, but kept promising they'd move me into the meat department as a meat cutter. But it never panned out. So I quit after a short stay at Berliner and Marx."

He filled out an application at the post office in 1971 and was hired as a substitute clerk, starting out on a permanent job with a one-year probation. His job was sorting the mail so he had to know the "scheme".

Because a lot of the zip codes on letters were wrong, he had to memorize the addresses and not go by the zip codes. This meant he had to take the "scheme" test. Charlie was given 100 cards with addresses, to be put in the proper boxes. He was allowed only five mistakes out of the 100 cards.

The first time he took the test, Charlie didn't study the scheme looseleaf book with the addresses they had given him, and ended up with five right and 95 wrong! As a result, he was told that in 30 days they would test him again, and if he did not pass that time, he would be subject to termination.

Sitting at a desk, doing paper work and juggling figures, was not Charlie's bag. For some people, it was their passion, but not for Charlie. So he saw the shop union representative and told him he'd rather unload trucks than do paper work. It was more to his liking.

"The union rep said, 'We'll fix it for you, Charlie. We'll transfer you. They're not going to touch you.'

"Although I was a member of the union, they didn't do anything for me. The post office finally went on a wildcat strike and they had to bring in the National Guard to sort the mail.

"I wanted to go on a week's vacation but the post office wouldn't allow it, as I didn't have any seniority. So I told them, 'I quit. I'm not going to stay with you guys.'

"My parents were upset with me because I quit a permanent Civil Service job at the U.S. Post Office. They thought it was a very foolish thing for me to do. For months I knocked around from one job to another, often questioning God about His destiny for my life.

In March, 1972 he again felt a need to go see his favorite Lady in New York harbor, Miss Liberty.

"I took the Circle Line boat early one morning. About half the way over, a thought entered my mind, *'Instead of going up to the crown which I had done several times, why not ask for a job?'*

"I felt strangely moved that this could be the Holy Spirit speaking to me, but I didn't think I had a chance of working at the Statue of Liberty. That would be like a Cinderella story, like a dream come true.

"When the Circle Line ferry landed at Liberty Island, I walked up to the administration building, and told the young lady at the desk I was looking for a job. She handed me an application for employment.

"She then introduced me to a ranger, named John Heet, chief of protection, who looked over my application and ushered me into his office for an interview. He liked what I said in the interview and told me, 'Maybe you can work for me as a protection ranger.'

"I said, 'O, I would love that.' I told him I was a Vietnam veteran, had been wounded and was awarded a Purple Heart. He said, 'Then you're a ten-point veteran.' I said, 'Yes, that's right.'

" 'I'll get in touch with you," he said. A week later, I called him. He was very nice and honest with me. He said, 'Right now, there's a freeze on and I can't hire anybody for my staff, but I don't think there's a freeze on for the maintenance department. Why don't you come back to Liberty Island, and I will introduce you to the chief of maintenance, Joe Rostick?'

"The next day he introduced me to Mr. Rostick, the chief of maintenance. He liked the way I talked. He asked me, 'Now are you a hard worker? Because I like my people to be willing to do any kind of a job.'

"I said, 'Mr. Rostick, you hire me and you won't regret it. I'll work very hard.'

"And so, sure enough, after going through personnel at Federal Hall, an office on Wall Street, I was hired for four months at a 700 hour trial appointment with the maintenance crew.

"I was so excited. I said to myself, 'I am going to work so hard that even if they don't make me permanent, I will leave my mark at the Statue of Liberty even if only for a short time. But of course I wanted it to be permanent.' "

EIGHT

1972 — What a Year!

"My first day at work was on Monday, March 22, 1972. I'll never forget that morning. I walked into the Coast Guard shack next to the Staten Island ferry terminal, gave them my name, and they replied, 'The guard said you were coming. Welcome aboard.' "

On his previous trip to the Statue, Charlie traveled the 15-minute ride from Battery Park to Liberty Island on the Circle Line "Miss Liberty" boat with a load of 800 passengers. Now, an employee, he boarded the smaller Liberty #2 staff boat with 20 passengers at the most.

"I was so excited. I stood on the bow all the way over, with my eyes fixed on Lady Liberty! My heart was beating rapidly as the reality of the moment was beginning to sink in. I was actually going to work at the Statue of Liberty instead of visiting her!"

For the first two weeks, every morning the young veteran stood proudly on that bow, with the fresh breeze of "Liberty" in his face and words of praise on his lips. And when the boat landed, he hit the ground running!

Charlie was assigned to groundskeeping—cutting grass with a push mower, riding a tractor to mow the main lawns, trimming shrubs, pruning trees, picking up garbage, changing garbage cans, painting, raking leaves — you name it, he did it!

"I worked very, very hard, at times almost to the point of exhaustion. I was determined to make my mark at the Statue. Sure enough, my supervisor, Ernie MacLarin, was impressed with my work from the start, and Willie Redicks, who trained me, told me, 'Charlie, I know you're working hard, and if I have anything to do with it, I want to make sure you're permanent on staff.'"

Charlie was encouraged. Soon he was working in mechanics, fixing chain-link fences, doing carpentry work, digging ditches, pick and shovel work, and plumbing. He was doing what he did best, physical labor and working with his hands. Though it was hard work, he loved the challenge.

After a few weeks, he volunteered to sweep the spiral stairs, all 168 of them, up to the crown of the Statue. His bosses soon found out that this amazing young worker had a special love for Lady Liberty. So they assigned him to work in the Statue in the mornings and on the grounds the rest of the day.

"I was dying to go up in the Torch but they said no one was allowed up there, except to change light bulbs. I found out they didn't have a steady man in charge of its maintenance. So one day, after I had been employed one month, I told a co-worker, 'Leroy, let's go to the Torch!'

"Leroy took me up as far as the gate that opened to the 42-foot ladder, inside the Lady's right arm, leading to the Torch. By now it was lunch time, and the Statue was filled with tourists, so I closed the gate from the inside, secured it with a chain and lock so visitors could not get in."

Charlie began his climb up the ladder, the original one, there since 1886 — up 54 rungs, 15 inches apart. Then, standing on a tiny half-moon shaped steel platform, he turned left, climbed a 7 foot ladder, and opened the door — to the small outdoor platform surrounding the base of the Flame!

"My heart was pounding real fast as I opened the door. I had wanted to be up in that Torch since I was a little boy. It was like I was the first one to set foot on another planet — so awe-inspiring!! The view was absolutely overwhelming!

"I looked to the east — the magnificent, beautiful skyline, with the East River and the three bridges — Brooklyn Bridge, Manhattan Bridge and Williamsburgh Bridge, and the Manhattan skyline.

"To the left was the Hudson River, the beautiful George Washington Bridge, and before me, Ellis Island. To the extreme right was Governor's Island, the biggest Coast Guard base in the world."

Ellis Island was the first port of call for 12 million immigrants to the States from 1892 to 1954. It was only used sporadically in later years. Over a million people entered the U.S. through Ellis Island in 1907, the peak year of immigration. The first thing they saw when they entered the Narrows, leading into the New York harbor, was Lady Liberty!

"And then, stretched out before me to the west, were Brooklyn and Staten Island, and to the back of that were Jersey City and Liberty State Park which was being developed.

"So there I was, on April 24, 1972, my first trip to

the Torch. I knelt down on that platform and praised God for His love and mercy, for granting this answer to my prayer of years ago to be up in the Torch one time.

"I resolved that if I were going to be there on temporary assignment for four months, I would go up to the Torch as often as I could. I might not have that opportunity ever again!"

For the next three weeks, there were two work crews on duty at the Statue, one starting at 7:00 a.m. and the other at 7:45 a.m.. Charlie was on the earlier one, so he came to work at 7 o'clock, climbing from the bottom of the pedestal to the top of the Torch without taking the elevator. He did that every morning for three straight weeks, starting the day with a half hour in prayer.

"I had a very strong feeling that God was going to do great things with my life. I prayed, *'Lord, please make it possible for me to be permanent here, and I will work hard to glorify You!'* "

At the end of Charlie's trial period, he received the good news that he was made a permanent employee, subject to one year's probation. He rejoiced, saying to himself, "They don't have a steady person taking care of the Torch. Different ones go up there once a month, and all they do is change light bulbs. I could be 'Keeper of the Flame!' "

At that time, a young lady, Jean Pearlstein, joined the staff at the Statue, She was fascinated by Charlie's attitude and his unique position as "Keeper of the Flame." Some of her college friends majoring in journalism became interested in making a documentary film of him on the job.

With the Park Service Superintendent's permission, they made the film, part of it at the American Museum of Immigration on Ellis Island. Charlie commented, "I felt like a real celebrity. Tourists even stopped to watch the interview. I don't know if those college students ever used the film, but it gave them experience. It also gave me a confidence in handling myself before a camera. This was to help me in years to come."

Charlie began looking into the condition of the Torch. He was shocked at what he found.

"The inside of the copper and glass Flame was filthy. It had never been cleaned or washed! Under the skylight was a lighthouse reflector with a 500-watt bulb. In the interior of the Flame, surrounding the glass reflector, were eleven huge 1,000-watt bulbs!

"Running into the tip of the Flame itself was a pipe wired in the junction box. It had one 150-watt lamp to light up the tip of the Flame, along with two emergency aircraft warning lights in case the power went out.

"There was a lot up there that looked neglected. It needed a lot of attention. I started washing the glass down on my own and soon I was changing light bulbs. I was doing quite a bit, spending a lot of time there.

"The word got out about what I was doing. When the Protection Officer heard about it, he told me I wasn't supposed to be doing that — there would be no more of my going up to the Torch.

"I felt shattered. I immediately made an appointment to see Superintendent James Batman through the Chief of Maintenance Howard Crane who was a 30-year veteran of government service. He and his wife were wonderful Christian people.

"Mr. Crane liked me a lot because I worked hard. I had that work ethic that he admired. And he liked my religious beliefs.

"He sat me down with Superintendent James

Batman who also liked the work I was doing. In fact, he was the one responsible for my becoming a permanent employee.

"Mr. Crane said to me, 'Charles, we know that you have a fixation and a great love for the Torch, and there is nobody assigned to it on a regular basis. I was talking with Jim, and we both agree that you should be the man taking care of the Torch, keeping the interior of the Flame clean and changing the light bulbs.

"What would you say to your doing this, with no raise, no extra pay?"

"I said, 'Sirs, I praise both of you for the honor. I accept your kind offer.' "

Charlie became the official Torch Keeper, or, as he liked to call himself, "Keeper of the Flame."

"There I was, assigned to what I considered to be the most sacred part of the Statue of Liberty, the Torch which held aloft the sacred Flame of Liberty! That was a great moment for me, and I was determined to be the best 'Keeper' that Miss Liberty ever had!"

Mr. Crane found a tiny portable vacuum cleaner that Charlie could use to clean the inside of the Flame. When Charlie ran into difficulty in cleaning the reflectors in the Torch, the chief of maintenance suggested he use furniture polish which was in storage at the Statue.

"I'd been rubbing and rubbing those reflectors but there was so much dirt built up on them over the years that they had a grayish cast about them. When I applied that furniture polish, those reflectors got so clean, I could see myself in them!

"I was so proud of those reflectors when I'd look up at night and see the light coming from that Torch a lot brighter! I felt like that was a major victory! Thanks to

Mr. Crane!"

In the summer of 1972, Superintendent Batman called a big meeting of all staff members, announcing, "President Nixon will be coming here in September, as he and Mrs. Nixon will be dedicating the American Museum of Immigration. We will need all of you to take part in helping make this place look spic and span.

"Some of you will be able to do some painting, maintenance, mowing, laying sod and pruning trees. We have some rugs that need shampooing and general cleaning. As much overtime as you want — no problem."

The work started the end of July. Eventually the Secret Service began coming around. Staff members had to give them their full cooperation. Also, two teams of National Park Service Law Enforcement Rangers came from their parks to help in the protection of the President.

Charlie was flattered when Superintendent Batman and Chief of Maintenance Crane called him into the office to introduce him to the supervisors of the U.S. Park Police, saying, "Charles really knows the Statue and its interior. Charles, take them around and familiarize them with the Torch and as many areas as you can show them."

There was a lot of work to be done before the President and his entourage would arrive in September. Charlie did much of the painting of the spiral stairs going up to the crown and also the landing inside the pedestal, as well as on five or six floors.

"I had been helping do some work with the first curator of the Museum, Ed Kallop, so I was proud to carry out whatever assignment I was given relating to President Nixon's visit."

All the lawns needed to be freshly mowed and sod laid down where there were some bald spots. Charlie had a hand in all of that, including the pruning of trees.

Mechanics were busy making a platform out of 2 x 6's and 2 x 4's from which the President would speak. Seated behind him would be his wife, Pat Nixon, Governor Nelson Rockefeller, Mayor John Lindsay, Senator Jacob Javits, and Henry Kissinger. Two big platforms were needed just to hold the loudspeakers. It took a lot of work and team effort.

The day before the presidential party arrived, a tugboat and barges transported five big trucks and unloaded them on the docks of Liberty Island. They were filled with nothing but chairs, so that President and Mrs. Nixon would have seats for their 2,000 guests.

When the hour came, Marine One landed with the President and Mrs. Nixon. They were escorted into the sally port, the original entrance to Fort Wood, and from there to the base of the pedestal of the Statue of Liberty where they cut the ribbon, dedicating the American Museum of Immigration.

The U.S. Secret Service and Law Enforcement Rangers then led the way to the platform from which the President would speak.

Although the workers on staff at Liberty Island were seated out of view of the area where the presidential party and its guests were seated, they were able to hear his message.

"I enjoyed the President's speech," said Charlie, "because it was quite fitting for the occasion — very moving and inspirational. He honored the memory of the immigrants coming from all parts of the world. Many of them came through Ellis Island, and he paid tribute to their memory, their contribution and their sacrifices to help make America such a great land, a land that was the envy of the world."

Yes, 1972 was quite a year! The young Vietnam veteran had seen the fulfilment of many of his dreams — and there were more to come!

NINE

"My Holy Place"

On many occasions Charlie would hide unnoticed up in the Torch after the work force left for the day. Nobody knew he was there, and he knew if he asked for permission to stay overnight, it would not be granted.

People often asked him, "What's it like up in the Torch?"

"The panoramic view is breathtaking, especially at night," said Charlie, "with the Manhattan skyline and the bridges all lit up, and the ferries and boats going and coming in the New York harbor below. The focal point of Manhattan is the World Trade Center, with the second of the Twin Towers still under construction.

"As for the Torch, it's my prayer chapel. I feel very close to God up there. I remember when the crew of the last Apollo mission walked on the moon in December, 1972. I was up in the Torch that night. Looking up at the moon, I said in a light-hearted manner, 'Lord, do You realize that You have two astronauts walking on the moon right now as I am looking at them?' It was an awesome feeling!

"With the media covering seemingly never-ending stories of the horrors of the war in Vietnam, I always prayed that God would put an end to that war and get our soldiers home safe and sound. *'Lord, move upon the hearts of the leaders who make up the United Nations to make sure that the Communists pull out of the South. Don't let them invoke their vengeance and holocaust on the people of South Vietnam and Cambodia.'*

"I prayed for my family, my co-workers and for people of all faiths who were being persecuted for their beliefs — especially for the Christians being persecuted in Communist countries.

"I sang songs up there, like this favorite of mine:

Jesus loves the little children,
    All the children of the world.
Red and yellow, black and white,
    They are precious in His sight.
Jesus loves the little children of the world.

From atop the Torch, Charlie's vision of caretaking began to expand to other areas of the Statue. He noticed the broken shackles and chains at Lady Liberty's feet, and said to himself, *"Man, I want to climb on those shackles and see those chains for myself. It would be a great experience!*

"I want to explore every part of her, as is humanly possible. I want to know as much of the inside as of the outside. In order to do this, I must learn how to climb the girders of the inner structure of the Statue."

One morning Charlie climbed the spiral stairs to the second landing, about 70 feet into the Statue where the Tablet section was located. He soon discovered a mesh gate, with an opening he could squeeze through.

"I climbed inside the Tablet, the book that the Lady holds in her left hand, with the Day of Independence, 'July 4, 1776', inscribed on the cover. Inside her left arm, I made my way on a small pylon that led to the palm of her hand and her fingers. I could see the hollow fingers.

"Then, facing a ten-foot drop into the inside of the elbow drapery, I climbed down there and saw that all those areas were completely filthy. I remembered we had a central vacuum system, so I turned it on, using several sections of hoses, and vacuumed the elbow drapery! I covered as much as I could of the left arm, her palm and her fingers, and got inside the Tablet as much as possible.

"Inside the Tablet, I discovered a bad situation — three feet of water in the bottom!

"Then and there I resolved that I would become the complete 'Caretaker' of the Statue, in addition to being 'The Keeper of the Flame.' I was determined to see that Lady Liberty was cleaned up."

Toward the end of 1972, Charlie's answer to his need for an instructor in climbing girders showed up in the person of James V. Benton, a Vietnam veteran with the Army Special Forces. He had been hired as an electrician and all-round mechanic.

"Jimmy was a hard worker, a man after my own heart—a rigger and a good climber, a guy who made you laugh and, at the same time, gave you an incentive to work hard. Certain jobs were starting to break where we would team up and become a 'dynamic duo' working together!"

Their first job was to replace the cast aluminum decking in the crown area that was worn to the point of being hazardous. The Superintendent wanted it covered with diamond plate.

Using brown paper, Jimmy cut three templates of

the crown's platform. Quarter-inch thick diamond plate was ordered and one of the mechanics on staff cut the sections with an acetylene torch.

"Jimmy had tremendous knowledge of rigging, so we rigged up a block and tackle in the Statue's super structure. When he went out on that iron skeleton that held the Statue together from the inside, I could tell this guy knew his stuff!

"As a fellow Vietnam veteran, and ten years older than I, he became my mentor who taught me a lot on how to climb the girders. However, I learned many of the climbing knots on my own."

In mid-March, 1973 they fit the diamond sections in the platform next to the 42-foot ladder leading to the Torch. Then, after closing time, with the tourists gone, they fit the smaller piece of diamond plate perfectly below the windows in the crown.

The third diamond plate was larger and heavier, making it difficult to get it to turn into position on the block and tackle. But Jimmy and Charlie, working together, maneuvered it high enough into the crown to lower it down to fit perfectly.

Jimmy then connected the portable welder to the power in the circuit breaker box and began welding the three sections in the crown together.

"At one point, I just had to go up to the Torch to watch the performance from that angle. Every time Jimmy would weld, the flashes would be bursting from the windows in the crown, back and forth, back and forth! It was like watching a Frankenstein movie — an incredible experience seeing that from the Torch!

"It took Jimmy two hours to weld those three sections together. Then he welded his name and mine, and the date, March 17, 1973, on a plaque. I said, 'We made our mark today, Jimmy. For years to come, people will be standing on this new crown deck of diamond plate. We did it!!' "

One of the things Charlie enjoyed most was taking people on a tour of the Torch. Among them were guests of the superintendent, rangers and staff members who worked on Liberty Island who were always granted permission to make that visit.

Charlie made a good tour guide, presenting the historical background of the Statue and sharing personal experiences in his extensive maintenance work on Liberty Island.

"I especially remember one of the museum staff members, Robin, who had a handicap. The wrists on his hands were reversed, so deformed that he couldn't grab hold of objects like those of us with normal hands.

"For a long time he had longed to go up to the Torch but he was scared of that 42-foot ladder. He didn't think he could make it up there with his hands being the way they were.

"One day I persuaded him to try to make the climb. He had his camera. I said, 'Now look, Robin, you can make it. I'm going to be right behind you. You just use your elbows any way you can.'

" 'Use your hands to try to grab one rung at a time; they're only 15 inches apart. I'll be behind you with my hands on your back!'

"He didn't think he could make it, but I insisted. Sure enough, little by little, Robin started to climb that ladder. About three quarters of the way up, I knew he was going to make it."

He made it to the top where there was a tiny steel

platform at the end of the 42-foot ladder. Then there was another 7 foot iron ladder that led to the trap door that opens to the outside catwalk and the tremendous view of Manhattan and the New York harbor!

"The expression on Robin's face as he reached the top was like that of one who had conquered Mount Everest — a great sense of satisfaction and pride lighting up his countenance! I took pictures of Robin to preserve his moment of victory.

"Coming down was more difficult than going up. But he made it like a champ!"

Charlie liked to check out "hiding places" in his rounds of the Statue. One time he was cleaning the fingers of Lady Liberty's right hand that holds the Torch. They were all hollow, with iron armature supports inside them.

"I was cleaning them out, using that little shoulder vacuum the Chief of Maintenance Howard Crane got me. All of a sudden, I felt something in the inner part of the index finger. I reached in and pulled out a little piece of what looked like Saran wrap, but it was more like wax paper, folded very, very neatly.

"I opened it very carefully, and found the remains of a flower! I could see that it had been kept airtight and was well preserved. There was no name, no note, nothing — just that little flower wrapped so carefully and neatly, and placed behind the armature support!

"I neatly refolded the wax paper around the flower and placed it carefully back where I had found it.

"Apparently it had some kind of sentimental value or some religious meaning. I think it probably had a sentimental or romantic value.

"With no message attached, it remained a sweet memory tucked away in someone's 'hiding place.'"

TEN

"It's about character!"

In June, 1973 Charlie was privileged to work as a helper with two professional craftsmen in the partial restoration of the Statue — William Cranford, a blacksmith and senior machinist, and Robert Gilkinson, a welder and all- round mechanic, both from the National Parks in Washington, D.C.

Their assignment was threefold: (1) to reinforce the underside of the catwalk around the Torch, replacing the original iron supports that were in a state of disintegration with new steel supports; (2) to replace the original 1876 armature bars that barely supported the wall around the Torch catwalk; and (3) to replace all of the 80 decorative ornaments from 1876, one third of which were already missing, with shiny new copper ornaments.

"It was going to be a very physical, difficult and demanding job, but probably the greatest job I was ever assigned, working for these skilled professionals. To this day I have never worked on a job I loved more than working on reinforcing the foundation of the Torch!

"Everything I had hoped for, God brought to pass because I was always willing to do the most physical job, no matter how dangerous or difficult it might be. I always had the first choice of any job.

"A lot of people didn't want to do these jobs because they were really hard, physical, even dangerous and dirty work. But I was determined I would be the best 'Keeper' Miss Liberty ever had!"

To begin the assignment, Charlie was faced with a lot of climbing. Mr. Cranford arrived with gangboxes filled with prefabbed steel supports for the catwalk. Some were too big to take up in the elevator so they had to be carried up the stairs.

"I was the grunt helper. I had strong legs and made a number of climbs. But both Bill Cranford and Bob Gilkinson realized the situation and said, 'We've got to start pulling this stuff up by rope. It's too tough, making all these climbs up and down.' "

It was decided that the rest of the equipment would be pulled up by rope, and many of the old iron supports on the outside of the catwalk lowered by rope.

The first priority was to build a larger platform where the 42-foot ladder ended, just before the 7 foot ladder leading to the Torch door. Bill Cranford built the platform with room to work in that area, so that Charlie could begin cleaning out the dirt that had piled up over the years underneath the catwalk.

"They might have been dedicated 'Keepers of the Flame' in years past, or whatever they called themselves, but they had done almost no cleaning, maintenance or painting. The underside of the catwalk was entirely covered with dirt all the way around.

"In cleaning out the dirt I found a whiskey bottle

that must have had caulking in it in the old days. I also found some of the original strikers. Apparently the first lighting system was like a gas carbon setup. There were incandescent light bulbs at the base of the ladder, and a dynamo generator.

"These strikers must have been needed to spark something up in the Torch. They were black, made of carbon, and eight inches long. Bill Cranford said, 'They look like candles.' "

Once Charlie finished removing the dirt, emptying it into a 60-pound canvas bag, it was lowered by rope to the observation deck below. Then Bob Gilkinson and Bill Cranford began removing the original iron supports from under the catwalk, replacing them with new steel supports.

"Those old iron supports were all pitted and rusted, only about one sixteenth of an inch thick and partially disintegrated! I wondered how they could bear the weight of people on the catwalk!

"Bill Cranford removed one of the original iron armature bars that supported the wall around the catwalk and took it back with him to Washington to refab and use as a template to make 24 steel bars.

"We accomplished an enormous amount of work in that one month before those professional craftsmen left for Washington. I still was amazed at how skilled they were. From time to time Bob Gilkinson would crack some jokes, and we would kid each other. It was an exciting time for me and I could hardly wait for them to return in three months."

They returned in September. This time, because work had been done on the outside of the walled catwalk of the Torch, Bill Cranford informed the superintendent that the observation deck below must be closed to the public—the drop of one tool from that high could seriously injure a visitor!

The original armature bars that supported the walls circling the catwalk below the Torch had to be removed. This required removing the railings and wall pieces to get to the armature bars. It meant grinding away the existing rivets to free the original iron bars.

Two iron bars were removed at a time and replaced with new steel bars. It was Charlie's job to buck the rivets and line them up as Bill Cranford hammered them in place.

"There were times when I had to buck the rivets on the bottom of the walls. I had to lean out from the Torch as far as I could, without a safety belt, to get the job done. And every time Bill would hit that rivet with a hammer, the catwalk would move!

"Anyone troubled with heights would not have wanted a job in which he found himself swinging in the wind that high up. But I ate it up! I loved every minute of it! I had no trouble with heights!"

The next phase of the work was attaching the 80 new ornaments. There were quite a few of the original ornaments from 1886, still riveted to the Torch walk ballistrade, that had to be removed.

Bill had a very small grinder with a little rotating head. As he very carefully ground the rivets off, Charlie wrapped them in newspapers to avoid getting them scarred or damaged, and placed them in his old Marine seabag.

"Man, things began to look great! Especially the ornaments that were red and copper, shiny and new! Bob Gilkinson was an excellent painter, transforming the outside and inside steel supports with a fresh new coat of paint. He also wrapped chicken wire around the Lady Liberty's palm and fingers that hold the Torch handle, to keep the pigeons from getting caught up in the Flame, unable to get out.

"It was a magnificent piece of work those gentlemen accomplished. I was blessed to have had a small part in helping them. I learned a lot, and felt like we were a part of history, since this was the first time the Torch had been repaired and refurbished since 1876.

"Bill Cranford got permission from Superintendent Batman to secure a plaque up in the Torch with our three names on it. I got to hold the plaque as Bill tapped the rivets in place.

"I was as proud as if I had been in Washington, D.C., having the President of the United States pin a medal on my chest! It meant even more than that, because I realized that I, with Robert Gilkinson and Bill Cranford, had made our marks on the Statue of Liberty for all time!

"Any young person reading this story should be encouraged. Just about every job I mentioned in this story was back-breaking, very dangerous, very physical, and very dirty. It was God who gave me great strength in my body and great endurance. It was He who gave me the will to accomplish my task the best I could.

"I never asked about wages or raised any questions like that. I didn't even care about letters of commendation. I was dedicated to Lady Liberty, and I wanted to glorify God by my work the best I could.

"Too many people in life look for the easy way to do things. They just want to get by. But their lives are really dull and unfulfilling. To tackle a job that you know is going to tax your full physical and mental capacity to their limits makes you a better person and capable of handling even more difficult tasks in life.

"One thing is certain — when we leave this world, the only thing that we can take with us is our character, whether good or bad. But quality of character doesn't just happen. It is built step by step as daily we make crucial choices.

"Working on the Statue of Liberty became a big character-building experience for me. However difficult the task I was assigned, I determined to give it my very best.

"I feel that was reflected even in the cost of that extensive restoration. Bob and Bill, the two skilled craftsmen and I kept the total cost under $20,000, We learned that there had been one bid of $70,000 for this work!

"Now, whenever I gaze at that magnificent symbol of freedom, I feel myself part of all that it stands for — liberty, peace, hope, as well as honesty, fair play and love for my fellowman.

"Each time I go up to the Torch and see that plaque with our three names on it, I am blessed!"

ELEVEN

My "Holy of Holies"

For Charles DeLeo, the Torch at the Statue of Liberty was his "Holy Place," an awesome site where he communed with God in the early morning hours before he began his day's work, and oftentimes at night. But, he still refers to the Cypress Hills National Veterans' Cemetery, near his home in Brooklyn, as his "Holy of Holies."

It was three years earlier, a short time after his discharge from the U.S. Marines in January, 1969, when Charlie visited a club, called the Cypress Hills Conservative Party, located on the corner of Fulton Street and Hemlock.

"Being very much a conservative in my political views, I thought, 'Let me check out this club and see what it's about.' After meeting some of the members, I decided to join.

"One day, in a conversation with a member, we were talking about how much the people in America owe to their veterans, especially those who went off to war to fight for America's defense and freedom, and for the freedom of other countries. We agreed there wasn't enough appreciation or respect given to veterans, especially those who served in foreign wars, whether as infantrymen or cooks, or whatever their branch of service.

"Then I asked, 'Is there a veterans' cemetery somewhere in Brooklyn?'

"He replied, 'Yes, walk over to Jamaica Avenue, turn left and it's about seven blocks. It's the Cypress Hills National Cemetery. You can't miss it!'

"So one winter day in 1969, I took a walk that way and, sure enough, I found it. And, I tell you, the moment I set foot on that burial site, I knew I was treading on hallowed ground!"

Inside the gate was a roadway, winding some 500 yards through acres of veterans' graves on either side, to the top of a small hill. More than 20,000 veterans are buried there, some along with their wives and children. These departed heroes served in the Civil War, the Spanish-American War, World War I, World War II, the Korean War, and Vietnam.

"As soon as I walked through the gate, I saw a couple of plaques. On one was engraved this short poem as a memorial to the honored dead:

On Fame's eternal camping ground
their silent tents are spread;
And glory guards with solemn round
the bivouac of the dead.

"That poem moved me deeply. Instantly, I fell in love with that place. I thought of my Marine buddies who were killed during the same tour of duty as mine in Vietnam. I remembered especially the body of that dead Marine in Khe Sanh that I tried to wash for burial. That scene is forever etched in my mind!

"I had a really strong desire to pray as I walked among those thousands of headstones, and on up the hill. At that secluded spot, the trees moved majestically with a gentle breeze. There was a solitude on that hill that fulfilled my need to be alone with God.

"I thought of the verse in Psalms, *'Be still, and know that I am God,'* an apt description of that sacred moment."

Three years before the Torch at the Statue of Liberty became Charlie's prayer chapel, Cypress Hills National Veterans' Cemetery became his holiest and most sacred place of prayer, and still is to this day. Sunday is his favorite day to go there because the workmen are off and there are fewer people then.

For this lone Vietnam veteran with a keen interest in American history, there was a kind of camaraderie with those named on the various headstones.

There are a number buried there, identified only as "Unknown U.S. Soldier." There's a gentleman buried there named "John Martin" who was the last man to see Custer alive.

Second Lieutenant Mabel Lacey from Arkansas, who was in the Army Nurse Corps in World War I, is buried there, along with Marstella Unger, a lieutenant in the same Army Nurses Corp in WWII.

Three Congressional Medal of Honor awardees are buried there, each of them having received the coveted award two times—Sergeant Major Daniel Dailey with the U.S. Marine Corps, awarded for his campaigns in China during the Boxer Rebellion and in Haiti, and Captain Lewis Wilson, awarded two Congressional Medals of Honor for action back in 1886, the very year the Statue of Liberty was erected.

There are 22 others who had been awarded the Congressional Medal of Honor, and the 14 men and officers of the British Navy who perished off the coast of Sandy Hook on December 3, 1783.

"The list goes on and on. I liked the wording on the headstone of Private Thomas Roberts, killed in action in France, in March, 1918: *'Love So Amazing, So Divine, Demands My Soul, My Life, My All'*, from that beautiful, much-loved Christian hymn.

"I was at the Cemetery again on June 16, 2001, walking around up on the hill, when I noticed the name of a soldier's wife, Ida Lind, buried there. She had died on June 16, 1901 — 100 years ago that very day! I must have passed her headstone hundreds of times through the years and never noticed it before.

"I went down, bought a bunch of flowers, planted them at her headstone, and said a prayer for her. I buy a lot of flowers to place on the gravestones of servicemen in all our wars, and pray for them, including their wives and children.

"I'm especially close to servicemen killed in Vietnam because they were my brothers in arms in that tragic war."

One time Charlie had the privilege of raising Old Glory at Cypress Hills National Cemetery. Arriving there early one Sunday morning, he looked up and saw the flag at the top of the flagpole was upside down!

"I thought to myself, *'How could anybody raise the flag upside down?' That means either someone was stressed or wasn't paying attention when he put it up there.'* I untangled the line, lowered it down, took the flag off the clips, put it the right way, and ran it back up!

"I was really proud that, once out of my thousands

of visits to Cypress Hills National Cemetery, I had had the privilege of raising our beloved Stars and Stripes in my most holy of holy places."

While Charlie was still a member of the Cypress Hills Conservative Club, there were a number of girls Charlie's age in the neighborhood who were members of the club.

"I asked one of them for a date, and she accepted. I said, 'I'll take you to dinner, and we'll have a nice one. But first I want to take you to a very, very special place, Cypress Hills National Cemetery. I think you'll love it. It's really peaceful, and I feel very close to God there.'

"She agreed, although she looked at me a little strange. She didn't live far from the cemetery. I was supposed to pick her up at two in the afternoon, take her to the Cemetery and spend an hour there, and then take her to dinner.

"When I rang the doorbell at her house, her mother answered. I introduced myself, to which she responded, 'My daughter is not feeling very good. She can't go. She's sorry.'

"I understood. She must have felt very uncomfortable about a guy asking her to go to a cemetery on their first date! She must have thought I was rather strange, and I understood why.

"I really had such a love and respect for that Cemetery but there was no way others would feel that way, too, especially a girl on a first date. I understood."

Charlie also remembers the two brothers buried at Cypress Hills, John and Andrew Kurchey, both killed in WWII. John was killed in France on November 25, 1944, and Andrew on November 29, 1944, also somewhere in France — two brothers, in different Army Infantry units, killed four days apart in France.

"A Vietnam War veteran, named Leo Coleman, is buried there. He was a specialist 5, killed in action in a Vietnam infantry unit in October, 1970. He was born in 1947, making him one year older than I.

"I once met his father, Ted Coleman, at his graveside. Ted and his wife often visited and put flowers on his grave. For many years Leo's mother wrote some of the most beautiful poems in tribute to their son. Since they were Christians, she would always include the Lord in those poems.

"Ted, his father, would then laminate the poems and duct tape them to Leo's headstone, a new one each month. I must have read 50 or 60 poems she had written over the years. They were beautiful, very touching!

"What a book they would have made! A mother's tribute to a fallen son!"

TWELVE

Father knows best

Charlie was eight years old when he got his first weekly allowance — 50 cents. He'd spend it on Saturdays to go to the movies and treat himself to popcorn, candy and a soda. Then one Friday evening he saw a poor derelict, looking real hungry, picking through garbage.

"As I looked at him, feeling the 50 cents in my pocket, I knew in my heart that man needed it a lot more than I needed it. So I gave it to him.

"Later on in life, as I began to read and study the Bible, the story of the widow's mite came alive as I was reminded of that 50 cents I gave to that man in need.

"I believe my learning the blessing of giving played a big part in my finding God's favor in my life. I discovered the spirit of giving is a special gift from God the Father.

"Over the years, God continued to give me the grace of giving. I can't thank Him enough for filling my heart with the spirit of giving."

A year after Charlie was discharged from the U.S.

Marines in 1969, he began to receive solicitations in the mail from Christian ministries. One of the first ones was from the David Livingstone Missionary Foundation in Tulsa, Oklahoma, asking people to sponsor orphans.

"I sponsored a boy in India and a little girl, named Pak Min Sun, in South Korea, for $20 a month each. Now and then I enclosed an extra gift to buy school supplies, toys, etc. I was delighted to receive each child's picture and a letter of thanks.

"It was just a glorious privilege. Before I knew it, I was sponsoring a couple more children, and then, an African evangelist named Samson, in Zaire."

Charlie was soon giving to several ministries, helping children and widows in the Holy Land, a Native American child in New Mexico, Mother Teresa's ministry in Calcutta, and Catholic Medical Missions.

After he joined the staff at the Statue of Liberty, and made the Torch his chapel, it was there he prayed for God's blessings upon the ministries he was helping.

During that time, one ministry became very special in his life, "Jesus to the Communist World". It was founded by Pastor Wurmbrandt, a Lutheran minister in Romania, who had been persecuted for his stand for Christ, put in concentration camps and tortured unmercifully by the Nazis, and later by the Communists.

Pastor Wurmbrandt's appeal was for support for the families of martyrs. Not allowed employment, they suffered greatly from extreme poverty and almost unbearable punishment.

"I remember the Holy Spirit laid on my heart to do something special for the families of these martyrs. At that time I didn't have any money in the bank. I was just living from paycheck to paycheck because I was sponsoring eight orphan children.

"I decided to go to the bank and apply for a $1,500 loan. With no money in the bank, I was acting on faith. The loan was approved. I made out a check payable to 'Jesus to the Communist World' and mailed it special delivery.

"That was a lot of money. I had never been in debt before but I felt such a calling from the Holy Spirit to do that. God blessed me amazingly!"

In February, 1984 the ministry of "Jesus to the Communist World" featured an article about Charlie as the Keeper of the Flame in its magazine.

From his years in the military to the present, Charlie has given over $100,000 in free will offerings and tithes. While he was attending the Catholic Church and later, the Seventh Day Adventist Church, he was giving not just a tithe, but 20% to 30% of his yearly income.

One year, while a member of the Seventh Day Adventist Church, Charlie became interested in a book written by its founder Ellen White entitled "Steps to Christ". It showed how to lead people to Christ as Savior and Lord of their lives.

"One year, I gave out 7,500 free copies of that book on the streets and subways, and for a time, handed them out to men and women coming to work at the World Trade Center. I paid for them myself. Out of each 1,000 copies, 300 were in Spanish and 700 in English."

Charlie also gave blood, ranking among the top donors in the nation. He donated his first pint in 1966 at Parris Island, a second pint in early 1967 overseas on Guam, before transferring to Vietnam where the only blood they took was frozen blood shipped from the U.S.

"When I got out of the service in 1969, the Lord led

me to my 'Holy of Holies' in the Cypress Hills National Cemetery. That same year I went down to the N.Y. Blood Center in Manhattan and made five blood donations.

"Since you can give every 8 weeks, I have been a faithful blood donor ever since. After giving steadily for 30 years, I have given 170 pints of blood. That's 21 gallons and 2 pints!"

Charlie has also given platelets 15 times. They are a part of the whole blood, basically used in fighting blood diseases, and cancer. They contain a clotting factor that really saves a lot of lives!

Each time he gave blood, he would follow up his gift with prayer, either up in the Torch or at the Cypress Hills National Cemetery.

"The Lord has given me an amazing ministry. The more I give, the more joy He brings into my life, and the greater the blessings.

"If I were not a giver, I don't know if God would ever have bestowed upon me the ministry of being the 'Keeper of the Flame' at the Statue of Liberty, or made me known all over America and across the world through the media.

"It's really a wonderful privilege to be a giver. We need to teach young children this, that it is much more blessed to give than to receive.

"This doesn't mean all of life will be filled with roses if we are givers. In 1974 I went through some very difficult times due to the death of my mother from cancer at age 48, and then meeting a woman that I hoped would be my future wife, but losing her to another man before that year was over.

"My mother was born and had lived much of her life on the Lower East Side. During the last years of her life, she moved to the Cypress Hills section of Brooklyn. But, strange to say, she had never seen the Statue of Liberty. I'd often say, 'Come on, Mom, I'm going to take you to the Statue of Liberty.'

"Mom was a heavy smoker. I knew she couldn't have climbed the spiral stairs to the crown. But just to have had my beloved mother, Molly, on Liberty Island, looking up at Lady Liberty, would have been great, but it wasn't meant to be.

"Early in 1974 while standing on a chair, hanging curtains in the bedroom, she fell off the chair, landing on her back. She had excruciating pain! As the pains grew more severe, my father finally took her to the hospital.

"Tests revealed she needed a spinal fusion. They performed the surgery and we thought everything was all right. But, after a week or so, the agonizing pain returned. We didn't know what was happening.

"I had never been close to my father, nor to my two sisters and brother. I couldn't be close to my grandparents like I wanted, because they didn't speak English. But, it was different with my Mom; I was so close to her. It was terrible to see her in such pain!

"We took her back to the hospital. After taking Xrays, they said she needed more surgery. That time they found she had advanced cancer.

"The doctor told us, 'Hopefully, through radiation she could go into remission and maybe live six months.'

"Six months?!! I was devastated!

"Mother was in St. Vincent's Hospital, deteriorating fast. After work each day I'd meet with my father on 14th Street. We'd go to a nearby restaurant and talk.

"He became very bitter and felt sorry for himself, saying 'With all these nasty, evil people in this world, why does this have to happen to a good woman like your mother? Why can't it happen to them?'

"By that time, my sisters and brother were living on their own. My father and I were alone in our home. He was even bitter toward my sisters, 'They never come over to clean the house', he complained. 'They never cook for us or take care of us.'

"I couldn't have cared less about that. I could take care of myself. But his bitterness was more difficult for me to handle, because I was losing the most precious person in my life, my mother, Molly!

"I went often up in the Torch and to the Cemetery on the hill, praying that God would cleanse my Mom of her cancer, give her a miracle of healing, or that He would take her real soon. She was suffering terribly.

"Finally Mom became too weak to eat. They had to force feed her through a tube in her nose. She was getting smaller and smaller, wasting away. But she was a champion. Every time I went to see her, she recognized me and would always say, 'Charlie, are you eating? Is everything okay?'

"I remember two days before she died, she kept begging me, 'Charlie, Charlie, take me to the bathroom. I'm tired of being on the bedpan. Please, please do it for me one more time!'

"But the doctors had said, 'Don't touch her. She's not to be moved.' It was agony for me not to do that one last thing for my Mom.

"On Friday morning, May 31st, 1974, I went up in the Torch at 7 o'clock and prayed, 'Heavenly Father, each time I go to the hospital, a part of me dies. My mother's so young. It doesn't seem fair. If it be Your will that my mother not survive and not be granted a miracle healing for her cancer, just take her Home. Give me grace and the strength to endure, and my father and family as well.'

"The next day, Saturday, the phone rang at 4 a.m. It was the hospital calling, 'We'd like you and your father to come to the hospital right away.'

"I said, 'Okay' and told my father. It was raining real hard, so we called a cab. Neither of us uttered a word. We both sensed Mom had died.

"I was the first one to walk into her room. She was dead, and looked so different. Instead of looking her 48 years, she looked like an old woman.

"I remember the first thought that came to my mind was, 'My Mom has just died, and they've already put another woman in her bed!'

"Seeing my startled look, the nurse said to me, 'That is your mother.'

"I went over to the bed, and broke down, crying. Then my Dad came into the room. He really took it hard. It was a very devastating time for both of us!

"There lay my Mom dead of cancer at age 48, and there was I, only 26. I had lost the most precious, dearest person in my life. I would never see her again in this world. But I'd always carry her memory in my heart!"

A few months later, Charlie's father moved out. His relatives introduced him to a woman, not too attractive, but with considerable wealth. He married her and they moved to Florida.

"I was glad to see my father move out. He was a worldly, bitter man, and all he did was complain. I was glad to have the apartment all to myself. But I really didn't hold anything against my father. I only wished him well.

"Shortly after that I went back to work. One day I

was aboard the Liberty #2 boat, heading for the Statue with the working staff aboard, when my eyes suddenly focused on what to me was the most beautiful woman I'd ever seen!

"Her name was Michelle Borgas, a new employee, an interpretive ranger. I had always heard of love at first sight, but I could hardly believe it was happening to me!

"I had always been shy around women, but soon after I got to know her, my shyness left. I learned she had a boyfriend named Max, but she assured me theirs wasn't a serious relationship.

"I was hoping they would break up so I could ask Michelle to be my steady. On occasion I took her out to dinner at a nice restaurant, The Chateau.

"I was deeply in love with Michelle. At least 11 times I took her to the Torch to share my prayer chapel with her. She was only 18 years old, not very religious.

"I remember walking around Liberty Island with her one morning. This was before I ever had a newspaper write-up published about me as 'Keeper of the Flame'. I said to her, 'Michelle, stick with me because some day everybody is going to know my name.'

"When I said that, I knew, without any doubt, that was going to happen. I knew God was going to do great things with my life and make me known all over the world!

"Michelle's mother and her sister Bonnie liked me a lot. She even told me, 'My mother and sister want me to marry you, and not Max. And did I tell you? Max may join the Air Force.'

"I thought, 'O, I hope he does, because then it would almost be guaranteed Michelle would be not only my steady girlfriend but eventually my wife!'

"In November she invited me over to her house for a family Thanksgiving dinner. I was really excited.

"Michelle and her roommate shared an apartment in the Bronx. They didn't have a lot of furniture. So one day she said to me, 'Charlie, I need you to build me a table and benches for my kitchen.'

"I took a day off, purchased $100 worth of lumber and hauled it from the lumber company to her apartment. I made eight trips from the street to her fourth floor apartment, carrying the lumber.

"The next day, I took another day off from work and built her the table with two benches. It looked real nice. That's how much I loved Michelle. She knew I loved her, but I was too shy to tell her so.

"The day before I went to her house for Thanksgiving dinner, she was running the elevator at the Statue. She turned to me and said, 'Charlie, congratulate me. I'm engaged!' When she told me she was engaged to Max, it was like a ton of bricks falling on me, and me not feeling a thing!

"She invited me to the wedding. Seeing her marry another man, when I wanted to be that man, was devastating. It hurt me as much as losing my Mom.

"Suffering the loss of both my mother and Michelle within six months only added to my grief.

"But God's grace sustained me. I believe if I had married Michelle, I might not have been open to the calling of the Holy Spirit — His calling me to be the Keeper of the Flame at the Statue of Liberty. I might have lived just for Michelle.

"I was so deeply in love with Michelle, she might

have replaced the Lord Jesus as my Number One priority.
So I believe even her marriage to Max was ordained by
God the Father and was meant to be. My heavenly Father
knew best!

"I didn't hear from her for many years. I did hear
that her marriage had failed, and she was divorced. But I
still hope for the best for Michelle.

THIRTEEN

Hanging Tough

The year 1974 had been a rough one for Charlie. He had lost the only person in the world he truly loved, his mother, to cancer. Following that heartbreak, Michelle, with whom he had fallen in love at first sight and had hoped to marry some day, within months had married another man.

"Miss Liberty then truly became the only 'lady' in my life. I adopted her as my mother figure because I believed she had a soul and spirit all her own. Her presence spoke a silent, universal language of hope that every one who cherishes freedom can understand."

During his Mom's illness, Charlie had worked with Jimmy Benton at the Statue, and they had become a team. Painters were needed to paint the entire interior of the Statue's super structure, including the iron skeleton, the interior copper skin, and the pylons. But before that work could begin, there was a need to inspect the 1,800 iron armature bars throughout the Statue's interior, and thousands of 7/8 inch bolts that held these armature bars together, forming the skeleton for the skin.

Because, years ago, this same undertaking had proved to be very costly, Park Service directors felt they couldn't afford to hire outside contractors again. So Jimmy Benton, Charlie and a third man, Jim McLarin, were given the assignment.

"Knowing we were there to save the National Park Service a lot of money, and being physically exhausted when I got home the end of each day, helped take my mind off my Mom's illness. It was exciting having Jimmy teach me how to climb around the skeleton super structure. I looked upon it as a great privilege to work all over the inside of the Lady and learn new skills.

"The work was a real challenge. In the process I learned a lot from Jimmy, including how to set the hook of the block and tackle onto the girder and secure it. Then he would suspend me from a girder in a boatswain's chair."

After chipping away at the bolts, Charlie's job was to cover them with red lead paint. The can of paint, weighing 20 pounds, hung from the side of his chair. He would start from the top of each section and work his way down to the bottom, then start all over again at the top of a new section.

As Charlie moved from one section to another he would lay down wooden planks on the iron girders to use as platforms to hold his tools.

"One time I was at the 40-foot level inside on top of the iron girders. My job was to place the planks on the girders. Jimmy, 20 feet above me, was to lower me down off the block and tackle to the planks.

"After placing a few of the planks, I got careless for one split second, lost my concentration, and stepped on the end of the planks, sending me and the planks crashing down! They made a tremendous noise. I heard a scream from one of the women tourists climbing the spiral staircase!

"My line from the block and tackle caught me and swung me toward the iron skin of the Statue. Just before the impact, I put my hand in front of my face to protect it, and then swung smack into an iron armature bar!

"I was shaken up. My right hand was badly bruis - ed. Jim McClarin, seeing me fall, looked real scared. But Jimmy Benton calmly said, 'Look, let's go down. We'll stop the job for today.' "

All night long Charlie's swollen arm caused him a lot of pain. But, concerned that he might be replaced on this job that he loved, he went back to work the next day.

"I was overly cautious, felt uneasy about climbing, and had little strength to draw upon. Every time I grabbed something, my hand really hurt. I was pulling an 80-pound portable welder, when all of a sudden the pain in my right hand was so sharp I had to stop what I was doing!"

The next morning, on the early boat to the Statue, Charlie vowed, "I am going to start climbing all the girders and get over this nervousness about falling. I'm either going to be an excellent climber and worker, or I'm not going to work out there. I've made up my mind!"

"Sure enough, I became more confident about my climbing. The grace of God helped me overcome the fear of falling and I became a better climber and worker than before!"

One day, Jimmy confided to Charlie that he himself was facing some family problems, "But, you know, Charlie, I'd just climb up here in the morning, be up here half an hour, and all would be so peaceful. It was a good place to put my thoughts in order."

Charlie knew exactly that same feeling. "I was doing the same thing when dealing with my mother's battle with cancer. I began pouring my energies into learning how to climb those girders!.

"With the help of the Lord, I became an overcomer. The fall made me much more aggressive. I became a fearless climber. Jimmy helped me develop the 'Big Climb"— from the interior of the right sandal of Miss Liberty all the way, 100 feet straight up, to the Torch platform!"

Charlie eventually was able to climb from the bottom to the top in a couple of minutes, and down again in an even shorter time! To test his physical endurance, one night he stayed over at the Statue and made the climb up and down seven times in a row without stopping!

To face a different challenge, one night he turned off all the lights inside the Statue, and the climb was, in his words, a "piece of cake."

"I was a bundle of energy, like a kid turned loose. Lady Liberty was mine! Inside her body was the biggest set of monkey bars in the world. And I was going to be such a fearless climber and worker that I would become the best caretaker she ever had!"

The year ended with Charlie living alone in an apartment — his mother, Michelle and his father suddenly gone, never to return. Only an alley cat named "Chico", that he had "inherited" from Michelle when she married Max, was there to welcome him each night when he came home. Chico helped ease the loneliness in Charlie's heart.

"As long as I had Chico, I wasn't so terribly lonely. In the morning I'd feed him tuna, some dry food and a bowl of water. As soon as I opened the door at night, there was little Chico waiting for me to pick him up and pet him.

"A painful time for me was flying home from somewhere, knowing there would be no one to greet me. My friends would have girlfriends or family members to greet them. I had no one. I had lived most of my life in a world of great loneliness.

"But God gave me grace. I really believe this is the way God made me. He has given me the privilege and honor of suffering loneliness for the glory of His name."

After his discharge from the U.S. Marine Corps in 1969, Charlie began to sense a gift for writing, a God-given talent for putting his feelings into poetry.

In 1975, Christian Crusade, founded by Billy James Hargis in Tulsa, Oklahoma, featured him in its newsletter as 'Keeper of the Flame,' and included several of his prayers and poems.

"Seeing my story and poems in print, I realized I must have some talent, since that established ministry featured my writings in over half of its paper.

"In September 1975 I wrote a poem about the flag, called 'Old Glory.' It wasn't a particularly good poem, but that night the Holy Spirit prompted me, 'Charlie, in the morning take this poem to the newspaper, *New York Daily News*, on 42nd Street in Manhattan, and ask them if they would publish it.' He prompted me to take along a number of photos of me at work up in the Torch."

Charlie did not sleep the rest of the night. He felt God was going to do something great in his life that had something to do with this divine assignment.

"Arriving at the *New York Daily News* building the next morning, I asked if I could talk to a reporter. I was directed to the fifth floor. There behind the desk sat a middle-aged woman who looked like she could strike fear in the heart of a Marine Corps drillmaster!"

" 'What do you want?' she said in a gruff voice.

"I'm Charles DeLeo. I work at the Statue of Liberty. I'd like to see a reporter."

" 'What do you want to see a reporter about?' "

"I have a poem about the Bicentennial that I think you'd like to publish."

" 'No, no, no. They don't want to see you about that. You'll have to leave.' "

Instead of being intimidated by the woman and leaving, Charlie sat down and "hung tough". He kept reminding himself, *"Lord, You didn't bring me here just to get thrown out by this woman. I believe whatever You have in mind will come to pass."*

"Finally, she lifted the receiver, and talked to someone on the phone. Five minutes later a young man entered the office where I was sitting. He said, 'Hi, I'm Stewart Ain. I'm a reporter for the *Daily News*. I hear you have an interesting story."

"Yes, I'm Charles DeLeo. I am the Keeper of the Flame at the Statue of Liberty. I have written a poem about the flag. Is it possible you could publish it in time for the Bicentennial?"

He looked at the poem, "We generally don't publish any poems at all," he said. Then, thumbing through photos of Charlie up in the Torch, he began to show real interest. Pointing to a photo, he asked, "Charlie, this is you in the Torch? Right?"

"Yeah."

"You take care of the Torch? Right?"

"Yeah, I keep the Torch clean and change the light bulbs, and keep the arm clean as well."

"Are you the only one who does this? Are there other people?"

"No, I'm the only one. I've been assigned to the Torch since 1972."

"Okay, look. . . wait here. I'll be right back!"

"I started to get excited. I knew something was about to happen. He came back with a young black man, a photographer. The reporter said, 'Charlie, we're going to go get our staff car and head downtown to take the boat to the Statue of Liberty. I want to do a human interest story on you as the Keeper of the Flame.'

"Right then and there I knew the Lord was giving me my first exposure to the secular media, in the largest daily newspaper in all of New York and one of the largest in America, the *New York Daily News!*"

Charlie joined the reporter and photographer and headed for Battery Park where he called the new Superintendent, Luis Garcia, for permission to do the story.

When they landed on Liberty Island, Charlie gave instructions to the photographer, "I'll go up to the Torch, and wave from the catwalk up there. Photographers are not allowed up there, so you will have to use your telescopic lens from down below to photograph me up at the Torch."

The photographer took a lot of pictures. Then Stewart Ain waved at Charlie to come down for the interview. He told Charlie the story would come out in a couple of days.

"Sure enough, I bought a paper two days later, and there I was, on page 4, a large picture of me waving from the Torch, and an article about my being 'Keeper of the Flame,' under a heading that read, 'He Carries Torch for Lady'.

That one story not only introduced Charles DeLeo as the "Keeper of the Flame" to all New Yorkers, but ran in the wire services throughout America. People were sending him clippings from their papers, and he began getting calls from radio talk shows.

Talk show hosts from across the nation called him that night, wanting to interview him at his home.

"I felt all along that the Lord had spared my life in Vietnam in order to be the Keeper of the Flame at the Statue of Liberty. Now I began to see why God had kept me single.

"I decided to 'hang tough' as the strange pieces of my life were falling in place. God's plan for my future was underway!"

FOURTEEN

"Let Freedom Ring!"

In March, 1976 Superintendent Garcia announced to the staff at the Statue, "On July 4th the world's biggest celebration of freedom will take place right here!" He was referring to the 200th anniversary of the signing of the Declaration of Independence, the Bicentennial, America's 200th Birthday!

Luis Garcia had served in the U.S. Army. Born in Puerto Rico, he and his wife were a fine couple who loved America. Their children were always so respectful, a wonderful family!

He headed a super team effort in preparing for the Bicentennial, engaging the cooperation of staff, maintenance division, rangers, enforcement rangers, museum personnel, and boat crews.

A representative from Disney World met with him to lay plans for an outstanding celebration, one never to be forgotten. As early as April, they began preparing for a fantastic fireworks display to blast off from Liberty Island.

For the first time, the "tall ships" would sail into

the New York harbor, as part of a Bicentennial special feature called "Operation Sail." They were to be joined by American and French warships in saluting Lady Liberty.

Jimmy Benton, Charlie and the maintenance personel worked with a group of technicians from Disney World to help set the stage for the historic event.

Walt Disney Productions arranged for a barge to be brought over to Lady Liberty, loaded with 14 giant spotlights like those seen at a Hollywood premiere, each equipped with its own generator. They were evenly spaced on the grass, surrounding the area that was the site of Fort Wood in the War of 1812, now the star-shaped base of the Statue of Liberty.

A large American flag was to be hung from the Verrazzano Bridge, a welcome sign to the ships that would soon sail through the Narrows on their way to New York harbor and beyond. Charlie wanted to get a good look at it from the Torch, so he asked Art Hicks, he foreman, if he'd like to join him.

"Art was a fine gentleman, a deeply religious and patriotic American, a World War 11 veteran who taught gunnery in the States, preparing future machine gunners on B17s. He was a credit to the National Monument.

"I said, 'Art, let's go up to the Torch and be the first ones to see the giant flag flying at the top of the Verrazzano Bridge.

"Art's knees were in bad shape so we had to go at a slow pace to reach the Torch catwalk. But it was worth it to see such a glorious sight. We were told it was the world's largest flag. The Stars and Stripes never looked better!

"When we reached the bottom of the spiral staircase and walked outside, we looked again to see that prize picture of Old Glory. Instead, we were shocked to see that beautiful flag being whipped by the wind in all directions!

"Art, in amazement, remarked, 'Charlie, no doubt about it, we're going to lose it!'"

The six o'clock news that evening reported that the flag had become tangled due to the strong wind, and because air holes had not been provided in the flag, it was ripped apart and fell from the bridge.

"How I wished we had had a camera up there in the Torch. Art Hicks and I were the only ones ever to see that flag from the Torch before it was ripped apart! It was replaced with one almost the same size, this time with air holes to keep it intact."

A couple of days before the big celebration, hundreds of small private craft began to dot the New York harbor. The Coast Guard made sure there was a zone open for the tall ships and warships to pass by without any interference. Even the Staten Island ferry and the Governor's Island ferry were not allowed to run on the day of "Operation Sail".

A U.S. Park police officer walked about Liberty Island with a bomb-sniffing German shepherd dog, as part of the tight security. As the Circle Line boat landed at Liberty Island with a load of passengers, the dog was there to sniff out possible explosives.

"The morning of July 4, 1976, America's 200th Birthday, I was the only man to go up in the Torch, drinking in the magnificent panorama of this history-making event! I'll never forget that sight!"

"Operation Sail" began with majestic-looking, tall ships from all over the world, including France, England and United States, sailing through the Narrows, approaching New York harbor. They were joined by several U.S.

warships and two from France. As they passed the Statue of Liberty, each one sounded its horn to salute Miss Liberty, the world's greatest symbol of freedom for all people!

Over a million cheering people lined both sides of the Hudson River, including Brooklyn, Staten Island, Manhattan, Bronx and the New Jersey shoreline from Jersey City past the George Washington Bridge, to watch this breathtaking patriotic pageantry!

"At 4 o'clock in the afternoon the Statue was closed to visitors as well as to workers. I would love to have been up in the Torch to see the massive fireworks show that night but that could have been dangerous. As it was, I felt proud to have been up in the Torch that morning and been an eyewitness to such an unforgettable moment of American history!"

That night Superintendent Garcia graciously invited employees and their families to be special guests on Liberty Island to view the gigantic fireworks display by Walt Disney Productions.

Eight technicians from Disney World were on hand to man eight of the 13 mammoth spotlights placed around the base of Miss Liberty. To man the remaining five lights, volunteers from the Statue's maintenance crew were selected, including Charlie and an African-American, Grant Sanders, known as "The Big G", whom Charlie said was always a lot of fun to work with.

They were shown how to operate the generators. Directions were given on how to respond to three commands: "Lights on!", "Shine the Light on the Lady", and "Oscillate the Light," which meant to turn the spotlight 360 degrees."

"The show began with the National Anthem as

Miss Liberty was bathed in the fullness of light from 13 spotlights focused on her. She was radiant! The top of the Flame was highlighted with a deep rich amber color light — a really magnificent tribute to Lady Liberty!"

Responding to the call to oscillate, lights flooded Liberty Island in every direction. At the same instant, an awesome volley of fireworks went off in a massive display that hovered above the open harbor!

Each set of fireworks went off from a different level — some from the ground, some from the observation deck on the Statue's pedestal, others down by the sea wall!

One massive blast of color light patterns across the sky suddenly highlighted the Twin Towers and reflected in the waterways surrounding the Big Apple! In the wake of the fireworks, a white, golden smoke suddenly enveloped the Statue completely!

"The band started to play very slowly 'America The Beautiful' sending goosebumps throughout my body!! The smoke around the Lady began to clear, and in her crown new lights glowed with a bluish color!

"Several more volleys of fireworks and patriotic music — and a fitting climax! A low flying plane appeared in the middle of the harbor. Hanging underneath its fuselage was an American flag in red, white and blue lights. And then it was dropped in the water!

"This was the greatest single event and the most patriotic one I had ever seen in my entire life! I have never seen its equal since then!

"This one was head and shoulders above all of them!! And for me to participate in the patriotic program that Walt Disney Productions put on, what a privilege that was! I felt fiercely proud!!"

FIFTEEN

Poetry by Charlie

When Charlie was growing up on the Lower East Side in Manhattan, he had looked at poetry as something written by sissies. But after going through the war, and God sparing his life in Vietnam and directing him to be the "Keeper of the Flame" at the Statue of Liberty, the young veteran began to express himself in poetry as he knelt in prayer those many mornings up in his "Holy Place", the Torch.

He wrote this entire poem up in the Torch in 1976. He called it: "My Request to God":

Dear Lord, I do not want to exist in the world
without any meaning or purpose,
But to live in the world for a mission and a cause.

I do not want to merely survive like an animal,
to be satisfied with only enough food and water
and a place to bed down in quiet and safety.

But rather to live to contribute something,
no matter how small it may be.

To benefit my fellowman and to help ease
the great sufferings that plague the world.

But most of all, dear Lord, I want to live
to give You glory as You deserve the glory
of all the world and the praise of all
Thy children everywhere.

I want to do Thy blessed will and to know
the joy of serving You, dear Lord and my
Savior, without end.

And I want to be a reflection of Your Light and Love,
in a world ruled by hatred and engulfed in darkness,
throughout my brief visit on earth.

In 1979, the following poem of Charlie's, "To Serve The Lord," was published in an article about Charlie written by Dave Smith for the *Los Angeles Times*, a newspaper reaching one million readers:

O Lord, I don't expect to ever
have the faith of Abraham.
Nor do I, O Lord, ever expect to
have the leadership of Moses,
Nor the strength of Samson,
or the courage of David,

Nor the gentleness of Joseph,
or the wisdom of Solomon,
Nor also the fire and zeal of Paul,
nor the great love of Francis of Assisi.

But what I do expect, O Lord,
is Your calling on me some day.
What is Thy will, I shall do.
What is Thy command shall be my joy.

If it be a small task, I'll do it well,
 and praise Your name.
And if it be a great task, O Lord,
 I shall not fear, for You will
always be with me.

And I shall not fail You, O Lord,
 for You are all I seek to serve,
My God of Love,
 blessed is Thy name.

When the *Los Angeles Times* published the article about Charlie, and his poem, it ran throughout the wire services across America. Hundreds of readers from Texas to Florida, Maine to California, sent him copies of their newspapers, carrying the article about him.

Three years later, the *Reader's Digest* contacted Charlie, asking his permission to run a condensed version of the *Los Angeles Times* article and to include the poem, "To Serve The Lord".

Charlie was always amazed that the Lord would choose to open up secular newspapers to run his story and his poems!

On the popular TV show, NBC's "Real People", which featured Charlie in February, 1980, they had him recite the poem, "To Serve The Lord", and then used parts of it again when they showed him up in the Torch at the end of the segment. In the background they played the "Battle Hymn of the Republic".

A year later the TV show, "You Asked For It", filmed Charlie entirely by helicopter while he was up in the Torch and Flame. They also used his "Prayer for Liberty", with parts of it at the end of that segment.

It seemed like overnight Charles DeLeo became

well known! His story was featured on two popular national shows. On "Real People" it ran a number of times as repeats. On February 14, 1980, in a Valentine's Day special, his segment was the last and the longest, four minutes! It reached an audience of 35 million people on prime time!

Charlie reflected upon that time, "The Lord gave me that incredible opportunity to praise Him, to honor His name on prime time before millions of people! Many of my co-workers at the Statue were moved by it."

"Another poem is "Especially for Motherhood':

I wish the world were free of wars
    and weapons were no more.
I wish that men could sit and talk,
    instead of making war.

I wish to see a world at peace
    with freedom everywhere.
I wish to see a brotherhood
    where everybody shares.

And especially for motherhood,
    for mothers truly care
about the wars that send their sons
    to slaughter and despair.

"Here's my my most beloved poem, "Wonders", for the glory of God:

I see the wonders of the Lord,
    in everything I see,
But the greatest wonder
    of them all,
Is the love He has for me . . .

"And I love this short little prayer of mine, especially reciting it up in the Statue's Torch, and at the veterans' cemetery at Cypress Hills:

> *O God, You are so Big,*
> *and I am so little, and yet*
> *Your love and concern*
> *for me makes me feel*
> *like a Giant!*

"And last, 'This Lady Prays', written in her words if she could speak. I wrote this in honor of Lady Liberty's 100th birthday, October 28, 1986:"

> *My Flame though changed from glass to gold,*
> *now blazes out with brighter hope*
> *To all that are on Freedom's side my Golden Flame*
> *burns deep inside.*
>
> *For Freedom costs an awful price, for millions*
> *paid with their dear lives*
> *To keep alive the spark that lights the sacred Flame*
> *of Freedom's Light.*
>
> *My Flame is fueled by cries and moans,*
> *by blood and tears and hearts that glow,*
> *By all who dare to hope and dream and fight*
> *to keep me standing free.*
>
> *They speak to me of woe and grief, of bonds and*
> *chains and agony, O, Liberty, sweet Liberty,*
> *I'll always stand on guard for thee.*
>
> *Great God has placed me where I am, and*
> *fashioned me with wondrous care.*
> *He always hears my silent prayers.*
> *I have a soul. I care, I care.*

These are but a few of the more than 100 poems

and prayers Charlie wrote and recited over and over, in the solitude of both the Cypress Hlls National Cemetery and the Torch at the Statue of Liberty.

Charlie, born and reared in poverty in a tenement on the Manhattan's Lower East Side, finishing only two years of high school, fighting against the odds to serve and survive in Vietnam, attributed everything of significance to the leading of an all-powerful God and Savior!

One might call Charlie a "folk hero" whose segments on some of the nation's top TV shows were aired again and again. Articles about him appeared in more than 100 of America's leading newspapers.

But with all the hoopla, Charlie is still Charlie. What you see is what you get. He is a giver, through and through, with a genuine love for the Lord Jesus. In every trial and tribulation he faces, he is not alone.

Through it all, he emerges an overcomer!

SIXTEEN

"It's good to be home!"

"One of the ministries that to me was special was the Holy Land Christian Mission in Bethlehem. A short walk from its orphanage and children's hospital is Manger Square, with the Church of the Nativity which marks the site of the Birth of Jesus Christ.

"It was in this part of the world that God's holy prophets were called to service, and where Christ Himself called His disciples, later apostles."

Charlie began his support of this ministry by sponsoring two orphans and a widow in Bethlehem. In his letter to the Mission, he shared about himself and his job at the Statue of Liberty.

At that time, the editor of the mission's magazine, "Holy Land Pictorial News", was a freelance journalist, Jack Anderson, who immediately saw the makings of a good story.

"I got a phone call from this gentleman, saying he would like to interview me and take a few pictures at the Statue of Liberty for a feature story to run in the "Holy

Land Pictorial News".

"I was delighted. Just talking to this man, I sensed he was a very warm, kindhearted Christian. During the interview I could tell he was moved by my story and the unique role I played at the Statue of Liberty."

"Jack soon interested other ministries in running an article about "The Keeper of the Flame" in their publications. Once, while in Manhattan, he scheduled me to speak in a church in the Bronx. Another time, he had a publisher contact me about the possibility of producing a book on my life. He was always ready to help me.

"My Mom had been deceased about three years at that time, and my father had soon moved away. I knew I would never see him again. Just as Lady Liberty had become a mother figure for me, Jack Anderson became a father figure for me."

But with several months between phone calls, Jack was unaware of the problems facing Charlie. That year was to be a very traumatic one for the Keeper of the Flame, with a lot of ups and downs.

To overcome his sense of loneliness, Charlie sought relief in tackling difficult maintenance assignments at the Statue.

For years Charlie had tried to get permission to clean out the debris in the bottom of the Torch handle, but the chief of maintenance felt it was dangerous to put weight on that area.

"I was concerned with checking the armature bars, to see if they were being eaten away with rust. I also felt there might be some historic artifacts in there that would be of interest to the Museum. Finally, I got permission to go in and make an inspection."

"I was excited to be the first man to get inside the

Torch handle in many years, perhaps in its history! It certainly showed no signs of any cleaning or painting of the damaged, rusted-out armatures inside."

Without a safety belt, Charlie wondered if the pennant would support his weight. He braced himself by spreading his legs, keeping his feet on the closest armature bars, as he began to clean the debris from the section above the pennant.

He discovered that moisture had caused a lot of the dust to harden into dirt. Pieces of broken glass cut his hands and fingers as he kept picking out debris and depositing it in a bucket, later to be dumped into a canvas bag. The glass was from broken light bulbs in the Torch which had collected in the bottom of the pennant over the years.

When the bag was full, he called it a day and carried the 70 pounds of rubbish down the arm and all the way down the spiral staircase until he reached the fourth floor landing of the pedestal. It had been exhausting work.

The second time meant getting into tight quarters near the bottom of the Torch handle. Joining Charlie was a co-worker, Teddy James, a full-blooded Shoshoni Indian and a seasoned all- round mechanic.

"I was determined to clean all the way to the bottom of the pennant of the Torch. This time I wore a safety belt. If the bottom part of the Torch handle were to collapse, I made sure that I would not fall 300 feet to my death!

"I inspected the connection of the armature bars from the pennant to the section above it and found they were completely pitted with rust. The pennant part was the worst! I kept cleaning until the bucket was filled, and

Teddy quickly pulled it up and dumped it into the canvas bag.

"As I got closer to the bottom, I found original carbon strikers that looked like 10-inch candles. Then I knew no one had ever cleaned this area before. I kept on and on, contorting my body into a human ball to fit the tight area, my arms aching and fingers bleeding from the pieces of glass.

"I finally got down to the very bottom. It looked like a pipe was wedged against the drainage hole. Then, I realized it was a striker. As soon as I lifted that striker, the rest of the dirt went sailing through the drainage hole, and a gush of fresh air blew right up in my face! Mission accomplished!

"With the armature bars in the pennant eaten away by rust and completely disintegrated, it was just the grace of God that was keeping that thing from falling down and seriously injuring visitors on the observation balcony of the pedestal below!

"I was proud of that job. It had been a really exhausting and dangerous job, but it was also a historic assignment. I felt I had accomplished something very special!"

After finishing that job, Charlie found himself with a lot of uncertainty in his life. He felt so terribly alone, facing the grim fact that his mother, father, and sweetheart had all been suddenly removed from his life.

His story as "Keeper of the Flame" had made headlines nationwide, and outstanding Christian ministries had featured his story in their publications. But fame somehow proved deficient in providing Charlie any sense of fulfilment.

At home in Brooklyn, his next door neighbors kept

playing raucous, deafening music sung in a foreign language over and over, causing a maddening vibration between Charlie's open window and that of the neighbor's. This, too, added to the confusion in his life!

Charlie opened the door of his mind to a plethora of haunting questions — *Is the Statue where I'm supposed to be? Should I strike out on my own? What if I left New York? Is my work over as Keeper of the Flame? Lord, why did you take my Mom at such a young age? What is keeping me from fulfilling my dream of meeting the right Christian lady? Is there a cure to this loneliness?*

"I was becoming discouraged as the 'Keeper of the Flame'. I was letting the enemy dictate my thoughts. Many times I found myself beginning to act on impulse, without consulting the Lord in prayer and allowing the Holy Spirit to reveal the direction!"

A new Superintendent had recently been hired at the Statue, David Moffitt, an exceptionally fine, gifted leader, a man's man in Charlie's eyes.

In June, 1978 Charlie put in his resignation,leaving behind his job at the Statue of Liberty. His co-workers were shocked. Jimmie Benton couldn't believe he had done such a thing.

Superintendent Moffitt was very surprised. "Look," he said, "I'm new here, but I surely don't want to lose you, Charlie. You are a good worker, and I think very highly of you!"

"I remember that day I put in my resignation. I left and when I got home, in my mind I heard a voice, *'You've done the wrong thing. Go back and tell them you've changed your mind,'* which I did the next day."

Superintendent Moffitt said, 'No problem, Charlie. I'll just rip up your resignation papers.'

"I felt relieved — that is, for a while. Then, weeks later, I started feeling in doubt again about working at the Statue. I felt a need to get out of New York and maybe settle down on a farm or a ranch.

"So, once again I did the unthinkable. I resigned a second time! That time, I stayed home for a week or so, and then began to feel, *"Oh, oh! I think I made a big mistake! But how can I face my co-workers? How can I ever face Superintendent Moffitt and tell him I've changed my mind again?"*

But I quickly swallowed my pride and went back to the Statue. Superintendent Moffitt said, 'I've already sent your resignation papers to Boston. However, I will call the regional office and tell them to rip them up, that you've changed your mind.'

"I was so relieved. I knew I lost a lot of face, and the new Superintendent must have thought there was something wrong with me to do something like that twice. But he was gracious about it."

One of the things that Charlie had had on his heart to do for some time was to stand alone on the very top of the Flame. By that time, any one who knew Charlie, knew he was a guy who thrived on meeting challenges, the tougher the better! They knew his first priority had always been prayer and placing his trust in a God that loved him!

On a Sunday night in the fall of 1978, before there were law enforcement rangers on night duty, Charlie began an adventure some would call "daring" or "dangerous", but which this human powerhouse of energy called "a piece of cake"!

"Of course, I wasn't about to ask permission from my superiors to do this. That was understandable, because they considered it a reckless or dangerous climb. All I wanted to do was to be the first one to stand alone on the very top of the Flame!

"It was 11:30 at night, real quiet in the harbor below. I threw a 20-foot rope over the top of the Flame itself, tied one end of it to the railing of the catwalk on the opposite side, and pulled it taut.

"Without any safety harness or being attached to the Torch itself by a safety line, I shinnied up the rope to the top of the column that holds the Flame. Then I just reached up, took hold of the lower parts of the copper and glass Flame, and pulled my body up on top.

"There I was at midnight, standing on top of the Flame itself, able to touch the tip of the Flame! I hugged it, and also noticed there were two holes in it. I realized that was the reason a lot of water had been getting to the inside of the Flame, coming through the disintegrating caulking around the panes of glass. I also saw what appeared to be burn marks, probably caused by lightning.

"I looked from the top of the Flame on the outside down into the glass on the inside. The floodlights, stationed around the base of the Statue, were projecting images of the Statue, from all angles, onto the skylight! Overhead were the starry heavens. It was a fantastic night to remember!!

"At one point, the winds started to pick up. The Torch was shaking a bit but I stood there for 45 minutes, praising God and asking His forgiveness for my sins, for doubting His love, and for my betraying all the wonderful things He had done with my life as 'Keeper of the Flame'."

From cleaning out the dregs and debris on the inside of the Torch handle, ending up cut and bruised, Charlie had climbed to the very top of the Flame, standing triumphant where no human had ever stood before!

What a graphic parallel to his climb from despair and doubting God to a pinnacle of praise and repentance! Like the prodigal's return to a loving Father, Charlie had returned to his Heavenly Father and stood triumphant in the glory of His forgiveness!

"I had brought my problems upon myself, with my weak faith, forgetting all God had done in my life, and with my impatience about what He was going to do with my future. I had sinned greatly in twice resigning from my job at the Statue.

"But like my Heavenly Father, Superintendent Moffitt had twice graciously welcomed me back to the fold.

"From the bottom of my heart I was able to say, "It's good to be home!""

SEVENTEEN

A Higher Authority

"I had rededicated my life on the very top of the Flame at the Statue of Liberty's Torch that fall evening. While there, I had left a small plastic cross wired to the top of the glass dome, out of view of the public eye.

"That signified for me that God would hereafter hold the highest priority in my life. It was like a covenant I had made.

"My faith in God was renewed. I started to do a lot of praying during January and February at the Cypress Hills National Cemetery.

"One particular Sunday in February, 1979 I was up on the hill kneeling down by a big old tree. I prayed, *'Heavenly Father, is it possible that You would help get my story into a very large publication, or even a smaller magazine or newspaper? I will give You all the honor, glory and praise!'*"

The next morning Charlie went to work, followed his normal routine, went up in the Torch, and repeated the prayer he had prayed the day before at the Cemetery.

The very next morning Ellen Bishop, chief interpreter at the Statue, said, "You know, Charlie, there was a man here yesterday from a newspaper in Los Angeles doing some human interest stories of people living on Liberty Island. I told him about you, and he wants to meet you and interview you."

Arrangements were made for Charlie to meet Dave Smith, a journalist from the *Los Angeles Times*, one of the largest newspapers in North America. His job? Combing the world for human interest stories.

"Superintendent Moffitt granted permission for the interview, which turned out to be quite lengthy, but I felt very comfortable sharing my story with Mr. Smith. I took him up to the Torch and gave him a book of my poems that Jack Anderson had published for me.

"At the beginning of the interview, I let him know up front the vital role my faith in Jesus Christ played in my life. That didn't seem to phase him. He told me he liked my story."

The next day Charlie got a call from Dave Smith at the hotel where he was staying in Manhattan, inviting him to dinner in Greenwich Village. During the meal, he said, "Charlie, I read your booklet of poems. I think I'll use one of them in my article."

"I said, 'That's great!' We parted, and after finishing a series of stories in the area, this accomplished journalist flew back to Los Angeles.

"I didn't hear from Mr. Smith for a while. Since patience wasn't one of my best virtues, I found myself muttering, '*Dear Lord, did you bring this guy into my life to waste my time? What's going on?*'

"Sure enough (*Charlie's favorite words*), on April 17, just as I came from work, my phone rang. It was a woman from the *L.A. Times*. She said, 'Charlie, I work at the *L.A. Times*, and I just wanted to tell you your story ran this morning, and we all loved it! Dave Smith did a wonderful article about you. It was very inspirational!'

"I was flabbergasted! I said, 'By the way, did Mr. Smith happen to use any of my poems?' She said, 'Yes, he used a beautiful prayer called "To Serve The Lord".

"I said, 'Oh, of all those poems, that was the one I wanted him to use! Thank you for calling. It was so kind of you.'

"I hung up, fell to my knees and began praising the Lord. I asked Him to forgive me again for my impatience and for doubting that He would answer my prayer to feature me in this newspaper. I knew in my heart it had to be the Holy Spirit that led this secular journalist to select this perfect poem, out of all in the book, to include in the article!" (See chapter 15.)

Charlie wasted no time. He hopped on the subway to Times Square and headed for a newspaper stand on 42nd Street that sold out-of-town newspapers. Sure enough, they had a half dozen copies of the April 17 issue. And there on the front page was the headline, "Labor of Love. . . He's the Keeper of the Flame!"

He bought all six copies and began to read the article, which continued on page 19, an exciting human interest story with a big picture of Charlie in action and his poem, "To Serve The Lord".

The article featured Charlie's faith in the acknowledging of God's call upon his life to be the 'Keeper of the Flame', in God's sparing his life in Vietnam, and in his call to be a witness for Him and Jesus Christ, serving the Lord at the Statue of Liberty.

"Can you imagine?! One of the largest newspapers

in America, with a million daily circulation, one of the most prestigious newspapers in the world, the *Los Angeles Times*! The power of God moved the staff of that paper, through Dave Smith, to do a front page story on me!

"Not only that, that secular paper had not deleted or altered the part about my faith in God and had even printed my prayer, 'To Serve The Lord'. That had to be the will of God. I know truly that God heard my prayer up on my holy hill at the Cypress Hills National Cemetery back in February.

"If I had approached a newspaper and attempted to persuade them to do something like that on my own, they wouldn't even have answered me on the phone. They would have thought I was crazy!!

"God had sent Dave Smith into my life. His article was the best ever written about me. The Lord had inspired me to give him a book of my religious poems, even though I felt awkward doing that at the time. Surely God intended for one of my prayers, 'To Serve the Lord,' to be featured in that article.

"I remember Dave Smith telling me, 'It will be basically up to the editors to do what they want to with the poem.' It was evident that the Holy Spirit moved on their hearts to print it!"

That was just the beginning. The complete story, with the picture and the poem, ran through the wire services across America. It was picked up and printed in big newspapers, like the *San Francisco Chronicle, Houston Chronicle, Miami Herald, Milwaukee Journal*, to name a few, including well over 100 newspapers of all sizes!.

Through that one article, Charlie DeLeo, the "Keeper of the Flame" at the Statue of Liberty, became known throughout America much more than he had been known through the *New York Daily News* article some years earlier.

Charlie was flooded with mail. People wrote him in care of the Statue of Liberty, as the "Keeper of the Flame" and included a copy of the article from their local paper. They commented on how they were moved by the article. Some said, "I cried when I read your poem." A few said they had it laminated and were going to keep it in their Bible and share it with their prayer groups.

"It made me feel so good. School teachers wrote me telling how much they loved the story and the prayer. I personally answered all the letters from hundreds of children.

"A Greek physicist at New York University wrote me a letter, saying, 'Charlie, I was so moved by your story in the *Readers Digest*, and especially your prayer, 'To Serve the Lord,' that I helped translate it into Greek. It sounded so spontaneous, like a psalm.'

"Housewives wrote me, 'Charlie, I say your prayer every morning.' A lot of Catholic nuns wrote me, saying they loved it! "

Charlie received a call from someone from the "Real People" TV program that was scheduled to go prime time with NBC. They were interested in interviewing Charlie at the Statue and filming him for a segment on a future program.

"They filmed me in June, 1979 with a good coverage of me cutting the grass, climbing the ladder to the Torch and even on the catwalk around the Torch. They showed photos of some of the orphans I was sponsoring and interviewed a couple of my co-workers at the Statue."

At the end of the segment, the voice of Charlie could be heard in the background reciting his poem, "A

Prayer for Liberty," while the camera slowly panned from the bottom of the Statue up to include Charlie at the Torch. Softly in the background could be heard the dramatic anthem of the "Battle Hymn of the Republic."

"The filming was finished in the summer of 1979, but the program hadn't aired yet. Finally "Real People" called me and announced they had set an air date. They said, 'We are going to air it on Valentine's Day!'

"I said, 'You mean I have to wait seven months?' They said, 'Yeah, that's the date we are saving it for!'

"I said to myself, '*Man, what a bummer!*' "

As each month passed, Charlie became more excited. "Real People" had become a very popular show, climbing to a 40 million viewership! He could hardly wait for February and the Valentine's Day special!

"The day finally came. I held my breath as I tuned in on Channel 4 at 7:45 p.m. The program was to start at 8 p.m. At 7:50 p.m. came an important announcement: '*Stand by. President Carter is about to address the nation!*'

"My heart just about stopped beating, as I blurted out in astonishment, '*Wha-a-a-t-t!!!*' *After waiting seven months to see my segment on "Real People", I am bumped off by the President!*' "

President Carter gave his address, followed by another announcement: "*Please stay tuned for 'Real People', to be shown in its entirety.*"

"It was then 8:30. My heart started to beat fast. I didn't know which segment I'd be in. I took the phone off the hook so I wouldn't be interrupted in the middle of the program. Many of the segments were hilarious, some a little too raunchy for me.

"But they had saved the best for last! My segment

was the last, and the longest — four minutes! One must realize four minutes is a long time on a show like that!

"My heart was pounding as my segment came on! I was shown climbing the ladder to the Torch and standing on the outer circular catwalk, while they talked about the orphans I was sponsoring.

"I could hardly believe what I was watching — absolutely overwhelming!! It became such a popular program that the same show was rerun a dozen times over the years!"

During the next five years God did some miraculous, amazing and awe-inspiring things with Charlie's life. Sandy Frank Productions sent its crew to film him for the TV show, "You Asked For It". They shot the entire show from a helicopter, showing Charlie up in the crown. Rich Little was the narrator and Charlie recited parts of his prayer, "A Prayer For Liberty".

"All this came out of that small prayer I prayed on the hill at Cypress Hills National Cemetery that Sunday morning in February, 1979, asking God to get my story in a big publication."

Something incredible happened in 1981 when the Washington Post sent a photographer to take a picture of Charlie up in the Torch.

When permission was asked of Superintendent Moffitt, he said, "Well, we have a procedure. No one is allowed up in the Torch. But you can take a picture of Charlie in the crown or down below around the base of the Statue, but never in the Torch."

"The next day word came from Mr. Moffitt for me to take the photographer up in the Torch. I wondered why the change, but I took the photographer up and he shot all kinds of photos of me up there.

"Later on, I found out what happened. The photographer had called one of the editors of the *Washington Post* and told him that permission had been denied for the Torch shot to be taken. The *Washington Post* contacted the White House photographer who in turn contacted Superintendent Moffitt, saying, 'You <u>will</u> allow Charlie's picture to be taken up in the Torch'.

"He was overruled by a higher authority, and that was God. God had made a way to get my picture taken up on the Statue's Torch for the front page of the July 4,1981 issue of the *Washington Post!*"

E I G H T E E N

The "Priority" People

Three years later, in 1982, the people at *Reader's Digest* called, asking permission to use the *Los Angeles Times* story. They ran it in their February issue which was distributed both in the U.S. and worldwide.

From there it was picked up on the wire services and featured in the German language in *Der Spiegel*, the most prestigious newspaper in all of Europe. Letters began pouring in from parts of Europe, Asia, Africa, as far away as Australia, as well as the U.S.

"I even got a phone call at home in the middle of the night from a woman in New Zealand. I don't know how she got my unlisted number. She was a young lady who worked as a prison guard. She had read about me in the Full Gospel Business Men's *VOICE* magazine and just wanted to know if I really existed!

"We talked for 15 minutes. I shared my faith and the love of God with her and learned that she was also a Christian. A strange call, but she was a nice lady. I wondered what that phone call from New Zealand must have cost her! To think that one article had brought us together from opposite ends of the world!"

A letter came to the Statue from a Christian gentleman, a native of Nepal near Tibet in the Himalayas. He was teaching a group of eight children in his village about Jesus and needed a Bible.

"The Holy Spirit moved upon me to meet his need. I went to Macy's in Manhattan and bought nine Bibles, one for the teacher and one for each child. I packed them in a box, adding a note for him to let me know he received them safe and sound.

"At the post office the clerk handed me a form to fill out, describing the contents, I thought to myself, *'These Bibles are going to Nepal. I'm afraid the customs officials, being Muslim or Buddhist, might see that they are Christian Bibles and confiscate them.'*

"The clerk asked, 'What do you have in there?' I replied, 'Some books.'

"Write down what kind of books they are on the form," he said. So Charlie spelled out, "Eight books of inspiration and adventure."

He ended up paying $40 for the Bibles and $45 to ship them special delivery to Nepal! Charlie wanted to be sure they got there!

"Six weeks later, one day when I came home from work, there it was — the letter from Nepal! I was so excited. I ran upstairs, not even stopping to acknowledge Chico!

"Thank you for your generosity, Charles," the teacher wrote. "I just received your parcel. When I gave the Bibles to the children, their eyes bulged out! They've owned next to nothing in their lives, and now each has his very own Bible! What a wonderful gift!"

Charlie began praising God. "It was His power and the love of Christ that kept those customs officials from opening that parcel. But even if they had opened it, I knew God was able to soften their hearts if need be!"

A large part of Charlie's mail was from students in the States telling how much they liked the story of "The Keeper of the Flame".

A student from Ed White Elementary School in Houston, Texas brought a copy of the *Reader's Digest* article to her teacher, Mrs. Murray. Impressed by the article, the teacher suggested that each student write a personal note to Charlie DeLeo at the Statue.

When Charlie received the packet of 25 letters from those students, he sat down and wrote each one a personal "thank you" letter. In addition he went to the gift shop on Liberty Island, bought statuettes of Miss Liberty and coloring books about the Statue, and shipped them to Mrs. Murray to give to the students.

The teacher was overwhelmed with Charlie's generous gifts. Her students made a tape recording of each one thanking him, and all of them singing his favorite patriotic song, "America The Beautiful." The tape was mailed to their newfound friend and hero at the Statue.

"I felt such a bond with these young students. It's no wonder Jesus said, '*Suffer the little children to come unto me, and forbid them not; for of such is the kingdom of Heaven.*' They are His 'priority' people!' "

Charlie began to think of a special gift he could send them. At that time the maintenance crew at Liberty Island started work at 7:30 each morning, and it was Charlie's job to raise the Stars and Stripes on the flagpole at the base of the Statue to start the day.

The flag measured 15 x 27 feet. Usually when the

edges of the flag became frayed, the flag would be neatly folded, placed in a cardboard box, and destroyed by fire in an incinerator.

"Instead of destroying this one particular flag, I decided to send it to the children in Mrs. Murray's class for them to display at school, thus instilling a spirit of patriotism among the entire student body."

When Mrs. Murray opened the box, she said her mouth flew wide open! She was ecstatic over such a precious gift! An actual flag that had flown for a few months at the Statue!

Excitement prevailed as the news of the flag spread from classroom to classroom. Pat McCanlies, the principal, herself a recipient of the Freedom Foundation's Award, suggested the flag be hung from the balcony at one end of the auditorium for all 600 students to enjoy.

Students helped clean the flag and mend the ragged places. The *Houston Post* and the *Houston Chronicle* ran articles about it, with a photo of the students standing on the balcony admiring the flag below.

The Houston school board was so impressed they invited Charlie to speak to the student body, not only at the general assembly, but also in each individual classroom.

"I was flown there on American Airlines and treated royally. Impressed with the number of parents attending the assembly, I told them the real hero in all this was Astronaut Ed White for whom their school was named. He had given his life in America's space program.

"I met a gentleman there who was active in the Houston community. He called me after I returned home. 'What would you think, Charlie, of having a good, old-fashioned Fourth of July celebration in 1983, with you as our keynote speaker!'

"Sure enough, they flew me in on July 2, 1983. I met a lot of people, was interviewed on local TV talk shows, and written up again in the media. On July 4th, I spoke to some 35,000 people who packed the arena at Sam Houston Park to hear my story.

"My stay those few days was filled with incredibly wonderful Texas hospitality!"

The following September Charlie decided to sponsor a contest for the students in the fourth and fifth grades of the Ed White Elementary School. He sent the plan to Pat Canlies, the principal, who liked the idea.

The theme was '*What the Statue of Liberty Means to Me.*' The students were to write their answers in a letter addressed to Charlie and mailed to his home. He would read each one and pick the top five winners of the contest.

"Even before I received their letters, I bought and shipped the prizes special delivery to the school to be on display. A two-foot model of the Statue of Liberty was to be awarded for first prize, a French medallion for second prize, and three medallions in English for the third, fourth and fifth prizes. The medallions were in recognition of the Statue's dedication in 1886.

"I read every letter, graded them and finally picked the winners. The winners of the first and second prizes were neck and neck. A Mexican boy won the model of the Statue and his brother won the fifth prize. The second, third and fourth prizes were won by girls.

"I was told the awards were presented at a special assembly attended by the entire student body, along with the teaching staff and the proud parents of the children."

A letter from Charlie was read before the awards were given out. In it he wrote, "*To touch a life is special, but to touch a young life is really something. Young people are the hope of America and the hope of the world. They are our future!"*

Charlie felt so close to these youngsters that one day he called the principal, "I want to treat the whole student body of 600 kids to ice cream and cake. Enclosed is a money order to pay for it!"

Again, all of this was a result of that one prayer that day in Cypress Hills National Cemetery, repeated up in the Torch the next morning!

"You see, when God answers your prayer, He knows the end from the beginning. The future is ever before God, as the present is ever before us humans. And the big thing is: God knows your heart."

Complete strangers who sensed Charlie's compassion through reading articles about him, often looked to him for answers to prayer. They wrote or called him with requests.

"Whatever the need, I tell them, *'I'm going to take your letter, fold it, and place it up in the Flame at the Statue of Liberty. I will pray about it for five days, while you keep in prayer at your end. We'll believe God for a miracle.'"*

Charlie's life has been blessed by his giving. As a blood donor, Charlie provided the gift of life to many individuals he would never know. But on one occasion, he got to know where his blood was going.

He had been faithfully donating a pint of blood five times a year at the New York Blood Center on East 67th Street. When he got to his 50th donation, he vowed he would give it in the name of the Lord!

"I filled out the form and where it said 'Donated for', I wrote in 'Jesus Christ.'

The lady at the desk looked puzzled. "I don't think

we can do this," she said. "Don't you have a name?"

"I said, 'I'm giving it to Him. Jesus Christ is my Lord and Savior.'

"But don't you have a real person's name?" she asked.

Charlie replied emphatically, "Christ is more real now than when He walked this planet 2,000 years ago!"

She said, "I don't know if we can do this."

He said, "If you don't do it, I'm going to walk out of here and not come back."

She said, "Okay, we'll do it."

Charlie sat down along with other donors waiting to give blood. Next to him was an elderly couple; the wife Jewish and the husband Greek. In the course of a conversation with them, Charlie asked, "Are you giving blood for someone?"

The wife said, "Yes, my husband's brother fell down the stairs at his home in Greece and was severely injured. We are both giving in his name."

Charlie waited for his turn to give blood. "All of a sudden, it was like the Holy Spirit tapped me on the head. There flashed in my mind the words of our Lord, *'Inasmuch as you have done it unto one of the least of these my brethren, you have done it unto Me.'*

"I knew exactly what I had to do. I went to the receptionist and said, 'Look, could you tear up the form I gave you and give me a new one? I'm going to give blood in this man's brother's name.'

"And that's exactly what I did!

"I actually gave blood for Christ, not the way I thought I was going to give it, but in a much more practical way, where it would be credited to someone in need."

One of Charlie's unforgettable experiences in helping children happened around Christmastime, 1984. He met a Christian couple at the Statue whose child had leukemia of the bone marrow and was being treated at the pediatric center at Sloan Kettering Hospital in the heart of Manhattan. He decided to visit the child.

"When I walked into the ward, I was surrounded by boys and girls of different ages with incurable diseases and afflictions like leukemia and brain cancer. A nurse recognized me from NBC's 'Real People' TV show. She greeted me and shared, 'Some of these children will not be around for another Christmas. This could be their last one.'

"I began making frequent visits, got to know a lot of the families, and found myself reaching out to these children like they were my own.

"I visited a lot with a wonderful 7 year-old youngster named Sean who had leukemia of the bone marrow. I gave him a coloring book of the Statue, a model of the Statue and one of my National Park Service caps that is part of our uniform.

"Steven Panzer, 18 months old, had brain cancer. I'd wheel him around the ward in his little wagon, and although he was an infant, I got attached to him.

"These little kids would look me in the eye. They didn't want to see any pity. But it was hard to look at those little ones, knowing what they were facing."

With Christmas coming up, Charlie wanted to do something special for those youngsters. For some, it would be their last. He started shopping for all kinds of toys — stuffed animals, fire trucks, model planes, and lots of dolls for little girls. By Christmas Eve he had enough toys to cover the floor of his living room. He had spent over $400.

Early Christmas morning he filled two large canvas bags with gifts and was on his way to Sloan Kettering Pediatric Center. He managed to drag the two bags, too large and heavy to carry down the block to the subway, on and off the train and on a short walk to the big hospital at First Avenue and 66th Street!

Security at the hospital knew me and helped me get the toys to the fifth floor. The nurses were surprised and delighted to see what I was doing for the children. I went from room to room, shouting "Merry Christmas!"

"I gave one precious 5 year-old girl a stuffed hippopotamus, and her eyes lit up! I gave one boy a fire engine and another a model airplane, and dolls and sewing kits to the little girls. I also had Christmas stockings filled with candy.

"When I was through, I had 7 gifts left. I gave them to the cleaning ladies to take home to their children."

Months later, Charlie had donated blood for some of those children. By August, 1985 he heard from the nurses that both Sean and Steven had not survived. They were already in Heaven.

"Each Christmas brings back poignant memories of moments spent with those precious little 'priority' people.

NINETEEN

Trouble Makers

"What I'm about to report is unpleasant for someone like me who has devoted his life to serve our Lady Liberty the way I have. She has been a mother figure to me, more than anybody in the world. I'm not about to see her threatened in any way.

"One day in 1979 I was checking the floodlighting system at the base of the Statue. I looked up, to see a windowpane come crashing down from the crown. I could not believe what I was seeing!

"I heard a lot of banging going on up in the crown. At first I thought it was someone going berserk, or some kids playing around and knocking the glass out. I couldn't imagine what it was."

"At that time we had no radio or dispatch systems, so I ran inside to alert a senior staff member. 'Hey, George, someone is busting windows up in the crown. Better alert the rest of the law enforcement rangers!'

"Being inquisitive as well as protective, I ran up the stairs in the pedestal. When I got to the base of the spiral staircase, I took a couple of deep breaths and started running full speed up to the crown. Halfway, I heard more awful noise up there.

"I took another couple of breaths and said to myself, *What am I running into? There may be some terrorists up there with guns!* But curiosity got the best of me and I kept going!

"When I got to the gate leading to the Torch, I looked up and saw an Iranian woman on the stairs between me and the crown. She yelled, 'Get out of here! This is none of your business.'

"I didn't budge. Then she lunged at me, pushing me down four or five stairs. I was surprised she was that strong physically. Finally, I pushed her out of the way and was about to jump into the crown area.

"There, confronting me, was an Iranian man, threatening me with a hammer as if he were going to hit me over the head if I continued. With him were four Americans, busy breaking windows in the crown with coal chisels and hammers!

"I was really scared. I didn't know what I had gotten myself into. But I had the sense to say to them, 'Hey, look, there are people below. You're going to kill somebody, knocking those windows out!' "

Finally, a law enforcement ranger showed up and said, 'Look, Charlie, there is nothing you can do, nothing we can do.' He told the leader of the demonstration, 'I would like to know your grievances.'

He wrote them down. The main grievance was that President Nixon had allowed the Shah of Iran to come to the United States, to be admitted to the Sloan Kettering

Hospital in Manhattan, one of the top cancer treatment centers in the world, for radiation treatments.

They were maintaining that the Shah of Iran was like Hitler and was evil. They broke out the windows in order to hang from the crown four very large streamer banners in Arabic. Then they chained themselves to the windows.

We called the New York Police Department (NYPD) who cut loose the protesters. The National Park Service law enforcement officers made the arrests.

The next day the picture of Lady Liberty's crown, with those massive banners in Arabic hanging down almost to her feet, made front page news in the media.

There were six broken windows. Charlie, by himself, took the frames off those windows and had templates made in the mechanics shop. He then traced them on plexiglass, mounted the new panes in the window frames and installed them up in the crown.

"I was proud that I was able to restore my Lady's crown without having to contract outside labor. I counted it a real privilege!"

That same year, a couple of unwanted visitors were seen climbing up the outside of the Statue, with backpacks and climbing gear. They were professional rock climbers, and once on the back of the Statue, they started climbing up her drapery using big suction cups.

When they reached a deep crevice in one of the seams in her drapery, they used an aluminum wedge like a karabiner and fastened it to the Statue's skin folds. Their aim was to get to the crown and from there to the Torch.

Two thirds of the way up, they gave up because of

the irregular surface of the Lady's drapery. The cups just wouldn't hold fast to it. But they put aluminum wedges into some of the turrets in her drapery, hooked up to their safety line, and refused to come down.

The NYPD sent their emergency services to place outriggers, extending ten feet from the four corners of the observation balcony, with black netting all around. If the climbers had fallen, they would have been killed anyway. But the NYPD did it for insurance reasons.

The demonstrators came down later that night. The only reason they gave up was that it got very cold. They were immediately arrested.

It turned out they had hung a couple of banners up there, protesting against the FBI's arrest of a Black Panther.

"Superintendent Moffitt was concerned, so he asked Jimmie Benton to rig a scaffold on the observation deck. He wanted us to go up there to see if any damage had been done.

"We assembled four sections of a wide aluminum scaffold on the outside and climbed to the top. Thank God, there was no damage up there. We did find their wedger and were concerned that sooner or later it might give way, fall down and hit one of the visitors on the observation deck. We managed to lower it down to prevent that.

"Lady Liberty's safety and protection were our prime objectives. She is the world's greatest symbol of freedom to the 'huddled masses yearning to be free' throughout the world. We owed her our very best."

When Charlie was asked what was the worst thing that ever happened at the Statue, he told about the day the "Statue Story" exhibit was bombed, July 3, 1980.

"Joe Cadispati, Fred Morielli and I were doing a

plumbing job in the Museum area of the Statue. We need-ed a chain wrench, so Joe and Fred went to Ellis Island to find one.

"That left me, our foreman Art Hicks, and a work-er, Chuck Greene, in the Statue lobby right by the 'Statue Story' exhibit. *(Little did we know that, at that very moment, a bomb was ticking off behind one of the exhibits!).* It was then 6:30 p.m. Visiting hours had ended at 6 p.m.

"Art Hicks left to go to his office at the other end of the Island. Thank God, the air conditioning units were not working, so I said to Chuck Greene, 'Let's get outside and get some fresh air. I'm going to see Art at his office. I'll be back.'

"Chuck stood outside the entrance to the lobby at the Statue, smoking a cigarette. I took off to see Art.

"At 7:30 p.m., Chuck came running into Art's office, hollering, 'Charlie, Charlie, are you there?' I said, 'What's the matter?'

"He said, 'A bomb just went off in the 'Statue Story' exhibit in the lobby!'

"I said, 'Go tell Superintendent Moffitt that a bomb has gone off in the lobby of the Statue.' I looked at Art Hicks. He was scared.

"I asked, 'Art, don't you think we ought to get up there and see if we can do anything?' He said, 'Maybe we should shut the breakers down. There might be electrical wires popping off everywhere.'

"He and I ran from one end of the Island to the entrance to the Statue. As soon as we opened the doors, we could smell black powder and knew it was a bomb. The smoke was so thick we couldn't see our hands in front of us. The alarms were going off everywhere!

"With Art behind me, we worked our way to the

stairs, from the lobby to the first floor, and then to the entrance to the "Statue Story" exhibit. We stopped in amazement as we turned the corner. Most of the Exhibit was gone! Where the bomb had gone off, we saw a gaping hole in the original concrete wall foundation!

"Five. minutes behind us came Superintendent David Moffitt. The first thing he said was, 'O, my God! Charley and Art, let's get out of here. There may be another bomb about to go off.' "

After a few minutes three harbor police boats pulled up to the main dock at Liberty Island, with officers from the bomb squad and emergency services. The FBI also pulled up and began interviewing people working overtime about any suspicious persons or activity they might have seen.

"The bomb squad began going through the rubble. I said to Mr. Moffitt, 'Sir, when it comes time for the police and the bomb people to check the Statue, would you want me to show them around?'

"Yeah, Charlie, show them certain areas. We want to make sure there is nothing else up there."

Three police officers from the bomb squad, a sergeant and three other officers, one of them with a bomb-sniffing dog, followed Charlie up from the bottom of the pedestal. They checked all the landings and tunnels. When they got to the observation deck at the base of the spiral stairs, the dog stopped. He wouldn't go up those stairs.

The spiral pattern of the stairs may have confused the dog. On the other hand, he may have sensed something. Two officers went up the "up" staircase while two others went up the "down" staircase.

The sergeant in charge of the bomb detail said,

"Look, fellows, there could be another bomb ticking somewhere in the Statue right now, maybe even in the crown. You've got to realize this may be dangerous."

"I went out on the girders while the police officers checked the spiral staircases to the crown. I met them in the crown but, thank God, nothing. I took them up in the arm, the ladder, the pylon, and into the Torch, and they continued checking on the way down, but found nothing. That was a great relief!

"I knelt in prayer and thanked our Heavenly Father that nobody was injured, none of the visitors, and none of the Statue staff, and certainly none of 'New York's finest', the police officers.

"I praised the Lord that He intervened, letting the air conditioning go off when it did, causing us to go outside for fresh air, thus very possibly saving Chuck Greene's life and mine!

"God is so good!"

TWENTY

"Project Restoration"

Charlie's cleaning out the various parts of the Statue had revealed hidden filth, corrosion, and damage by wind and water. What he discovered as self-appointed "Caretaker of the Statue" and "Keeper of the Flame" may have sparked the interest in further inspection by professionals.

Whether it did or not, the authorities realized the time had come for a major overhaul of the Statue of Liberty. A massive "Project Restoration" was scheduled to be launched January, 1984.

Before that could begin, it was necessary to conduct a thorough hi-tech inspection of the inner super structure of the world's most famous monument. That began in the summer of 1983.

The people of France raised over a million dollars to send a team of their architects, engineers and technicians, along with 15 huge wooden crates of equipment — computers, calibration instruments, wire hook-ups, etc.

Their main job was to calibrate the strength of the

central pylon that runs from the interior base of the Statue to the level of Lady Liberty's shoulders, just beneath her crown. They were also to test the strength of the 42-foot iron pylon in her right arm, and compute the wind stress on the Torch and Flame and the area around her feet.

"Superintendent Moffitt gave me the great privilege of working with that French team of top professionals. Some spoke good English; most, no English at all.

"Two of the men I helped were hard workers — a structural engineer, Ramon, and his technician assistant, Claude. For 13 weeks we worked for days on end and often into the night.

"Part of the task for Jimmy Benton and me was to build special landings throughout the interior iron skeleton, from the feet of the Lady to her crown, and to connect them with ladders. On each platform we were to construct a workbench that the engineers could use to hold their computers and calibration equipment while doing their testing.

"Jimmy's tremendous skill in rigging and knowing how to set up scaffolding and planks helped in getting the job done. As usual we worked as a team, climbing girders and maneuvering 14-foot heavy planks into position by block and tackle.

"Once the platforms were completed, Jimmy's work was done, leaving me on my own to assist the French technicians. My job then was to feed spools of cable to the platforms so they could plug in their special equipment.

"In the process I was asked to measure a whole series of girders throughout the interior superstructure. It was a challenge — I didn't know how to read the metric measurements; and, by myself, it was difficult to feed tape from one end of a girder to the other end."

Charlie mastered the measurements by supplying the amount of notches past a given number. He was somehow able to handle the tape to measure the girders whether they ran horizontal or vertical. Ramon and Claude were pleased with the results.

After they had finished their calibrations and testings, their word was that many of the areas had maintained their durability.

"They were real gentlemen who showed their appreciation for the way I was able to help them. After returning home, they sent me a gift of a two-foot model of the Eiffel Tower, which I still have at home."

"Project Restoration" began January, 1984, a giant task that took two and a half years to complete.

Through it all Lady Liberty stood proud, completely surrounded by scaffolding, with teams of French and American technicians and workers laboring side by side on this historic site.

President Ronald Reagan had appointed Lee Iacocca as Chairman of the Statue of Liberty and Ellis Island Foundation because he was able to generate the kind of financial support for backing this huge undertaking.

In early January a barge landed on the main dock at Liberty Island, loaded with 200 tons of aluminum scaffolding which would become the tallest free standing scaffold in the world!

During the Restoration, most of the staff, including Charlie, were kept busy working on nearby Ellis Island, building offices. But this couldn't keep the "Keeper of the Flame" away from Lady Liberty!

"It was really a work of art to see those men erect that scaffold. They had nerve. Those guys were men after my own heart. I wish I could have helped them, but I wasn't a trained scaffold man.

"Back then, I was off Fridays and Saturdays, so every Sunday morning, no matter where they left off, I would climb the scaffold to that level, hand over hand, like the scaffold workers had to do.

"Each Sunday, as the levels got higher and higher, I kept climbing it. Finally they got the scaffold as tall as the crown. I climbed it, hand over hand, til I got to the level of the crown.

"At that point I walked around the aluminum planking. I was flabbergasted to find myself looking at the Lady's face close up! What a tremendous feeling! Outside of the scaffold men, I was the first one to see Lady Liberty's face so close up without being in a helicopter!

"One Sunday I climbed the inner scaffolding, and was ready to jump on her fingers which cradled the Tablet, with the words, 'July 4th, 1776'. I discovered the letters and Roman numerals were about two feet long and four inches wide. They were solid so I stood on them.

"I shinnied up on the Tablet, onto the upper keystone and sat down on it. I felt like I was sitting on top of the world!"

Charlie's dream had always been to explore as much of the outside of the Statue of Liberty as he possibly could. Another dream was to stand on Lady Liberty's head, but that had always been impossible without scaffolding.

One day he found out through the grapevine that they were going to hire private security guards to guard the scaffolding seven days a week around the clock.

"I made up my mind that before that happened, I would climb the scaffolding from the outside all the way up to the Torch, and jump on the Torch. Then, from the Torch, back down the scaffolding again, to be able to say, 'One time in my life I actually climbed the Torch and the Flame from the outside instead of the inside!'

"The Sunday before the security guards were coming on Monday was my one opportunity! I stayed overnight, put on my safety belt and started to climb the scaffolding, hand over hand.

"I got to the Tablet, and sitting on the upper keystone, I looked up at Lady Liberty's deep rich, amber-colored Flame. I remembered installing those sodium vapor lamps and that lighting system, with the aid of the electrical contractors, for the U.S. Bicentennial. There were also the crown windows where the mercury vapor lamps burned a light blue. I was proud of them!

"I continued climbing until I was opposite Lady's face, about five feet away at that point! Even as reckless as I had been in my life, I knew there was no way I could make that jump without a running start. I was thinking of trying to grab one of her seven spikes which symbolize rays of light illuminating from a 25-jewel crown window.

"I decided not to try it. So I proceeded back to where the Torch and the right arm were. When I put my foot on the scaffold, to climb to the Torch, it moved!

"I thought, 'What would happen if, when I got to the top of this scaffold, it toppled down?' But this is the only opportunity I will ever have to climb the scaffold from the outside, jump onto the Torch, and then climb down from there!'

"I climbed the section of the scaffolding, passing the right arm. At that point, I was about two and a half feet from the Torch railing. I didn't want to hook up my safety harness to the scaffold in case the weight of my momentum might have shifted that scaffold.

"I didn't hook up at all, but extended my arms, grabbed the railing, and jumped right onto the catwalk. It was really amazing!

"There I stopped and said a prayer that God would watch over and protect the men and women working on the restoration of the Statue of Liberty, give them grace and favor, that they would be able to work without being injured, and that we would have no problems with any terrorist group seeking to disrupt the restoration.

"A few days later, early in the morning, I climbed on top of Miss Liberty's crown from the scaffold, and started sliding down onto the scaffolding again; and then ran back up on top of her head and slid another two dozen times!"

"Charlie the Kid" was at his best again, and by God's grace "Charlie the Boy" was climbing all over the outside of the Statue of Liberty's body, thanks to the 300 foot scaffolding!

"I must have been doing 50 miles per hour sliding down the back of the Statue's head! I also loved sitting on all seven of her copper spikes or rays atop her crown as well! What a blast! It was awesome!!

"Then I climbed down to the crown part and stood before Miss Liberty's beautiful, majestic face. Her expression was one of peace, strength, compassion and dignity!

Looking back over the years, Charlie figured he had made the trip up to the Torch 2,500 times, not only by climbing the spiral stairs, but also by climbing the girders that were part of the inner iron skeleton.

"But to reach the Torch by climbing the outside

scaffold, hand over hand, was really unique. There was only the one time I could do it, and I did it!"

During the process of restoration, it was determined that the Torch and Flame had to come down for special testing. That meant disconnecting them at the bottom of the catwalk where Liberty's hand and finger were.

"As I watched them come down, I was almost in tears. I couldn't believe they were taking down my prayer chapel. I said to myself, 'I will never love the new Torch and Flame the way I loved the other one. Never!'

The new Flame was to be a solid copper shell, riveted together in so many pieces, with stainless steel armature supports on the inside to give it strength. It would then be covered with many layers of shellac, followed by the application of 5,000 strips of gold leaf!

It is interesting to note that Auguste Bartholdi, the French sculptor of the Statue of Liberty, originally wanted his Flame to be gold-leafed with outside lighting to reflect off the gold leaf. But the U.S. Lighthouse Board, commissioned by President Grover Cleveland to take care of the Statue, wanted the Flame to function as a lighthouse with lights on the inside reflecting outward to two rows of circular glass windows around the lower part of the Flame.

On the new Torch, there were16 copper light fixtures placed all around the 360 degrees of the Torch's circular catwalk. Behind each one was an ornamental figure of a leaf on the catwalk. The lights were 250 watt quartz lamps that reflected off the gold leafed Flame.

"It was a mind boggling experience to see it all come together. I realized I would be the first 'Keeper' in the history of the Statue of Liberty to be privileged to have taken care of not one Torch, but two."

The original Torch and the remodeled copper and

glass Flame were eventually moved into the lobby on the ground floor of the pedestal, the base of the Statue.

"In May, 1986 the new Torch and Flame were hoisted by crane into position and fit right in place. A salute to the great work of those engineers, architects, iron workers and scaffold workers!

"Little did I know that I would soon not only fall in love with the new golden Flame and Torch, but I would love them more than the old Flame and Torch!!"

On July 5, 1986 Nancy Reagan officially rededicated the Statue of Liberty, with Lee Iococca and other dignitaries present, opening it up to visitors after having been closed two and a half years.

The First Lady was the first one escorted up to the crown. From a helicopter a photo was taken of her with two children waving from the windows.

"I really admired President and Mrs. Reagan. I believe Ronald Reagan was the very best President in my lifetime and one of the best in American history.

"In my old prayer chapel at the Torch I always used to pray for the President, whether he was a Democrat or Republican. He was our commander-in-chief, and I always gave him my prayers and support.

"I prayed for Congress, the Senate, the Mayor, people in authority and school teachers, and for the homeless, victims of AIDS, and cancer patients. But my number one prayer was to know God's will through His Holy Spirit.

"That had been a good prayer chapel, but now I had a new Torch Chapel. Instead of looking up through the glass and copper Flame, I was looking up at the golden Flame. And I had already begun to love that beautiful golden Flame!"

TWENTY ONE

Charlie on PARADE!

"In the early part of 1990, I got a call from a writer, Christopher Phillips, who said he'd like to do a feature on me for the *Reader's Digest*. I said, 'O, that's great!'

"Two days before he came to interview me on Liberty Island, he called me again, and I told him, 'In 1982 I was featured in the *Reader's Digest*, a reprint from the earlier *Los Angeles Times* story.'

"He said, 'O, well, then they might not want to do another story on you. But I'll get back to you.'

"I said to myself, *'Dear Lord, why didn't I keep my mouth shut?'*

"But God knew He had something more exciting for me. Mr. Phillips called me back again, and said, 'Charlie, have you ever been in *PARADE* magazine?' I said, 'No,' and my eyes popped open wide! *PARADE* was a publication with 40 million readers!

"Christopher said, 'Well, I talked to them about you, and they seem to be very interested in doing a feature on you.'

"I said, 'Christopher, just a year ago I was the first man ever to climb on top of the golden Flame. I was there to wash down the seagull droppings. You can tell *PARADE* that, if they're willing to charter a helicopter, I can climb on top of the Flame early in the morning and they can take some nice pictures. From them they can get a good cover shot.'

"He got excited right away. The next night he called me back, 'Charlie, they went crazy over the idea of photographing you standing on top of the golden Flame!'

"I said, 'I'll even bring a flag with me and wave it up there! You said this story was possibly for the July 4th issue. Stars and stripes and Lady Liberty go mighty good together — like peanut butter and jelly!' "

Charlie knew he could get permission for the interview, but he also knew he would never be granted permission for the photo shot of him atop the golden Flame.

"The Lord had spared my life in Vietnam and had guided me to be the Keeper of the Flame at the Statue of Liberty. I had been the Keeper of the Flame for 18 years, and I had done a lot of difficult and dangerous work. My body was starting to show wear and tear."

Without the aid of a scaffold, Charlie had single-handedly kept the entire interior of the Statue of Liberty's superstructure spotlessly clean — 70,000 cubic feet of the interior skin! And, although he would call every job he took on a "piece of cake", there were many dangerous assignments. One slip and he could have been gone!

Having Charlie on top of the Flame with no scaffolding in place would put the National Park Service in a difficult position. It could be said, "You are asking your employees to do hazardous work. What's he doing standing there on the golden Flame?"

"I knew I would get some kind of reprimand, but I prayed, '*Lord, if this is Your will, just keep alive the desire for me to do this, and I will take that as a sign it is Your will. If it is not Your will for me to pose on top of the golden Flame, then through Your Holy Spirit let me know.*'

"But the desire had always been very strong. Six years before, I had written to *PARADE* magazine asking if they'd be interested in doing an interview with me but I never heard from them.

"Isn't God wonderful! He knew that to stand on that Flame was one of the desires of my heart, and now I had done it! Now *PARADE* magazine was asking me for an interview!

"That day in May, 1989, when I went up to make a routine inspection of the lights in the Torch, I saw the hits on the golden Flame made by large amounts of seagull droppings. I believe that the Lord directed those seagulls over the Flame, just to do what they did!

"Because that was when I climbed atop the Flame and stood there for the first time!"

When Christopher Phillips came for the interview at the Statue, Charlie outlined the plan: "I will stay overnight on Liberty Island. Early in the morning, about 5:45 a.m., before the boat comes with the morning staff, I'll be up at the Torch.

"I'll be standing on top of the golden Flame at about 6:05 a.m. I'll want the helicopter with the photographer in it to come by no later than 6:10. I am only going to be able to give you a half hour of my time, posing on top of the Flame from 6:15 to 6:45.

"I want it to be the most dramatic picture possible! At 6:45, whether the photographer is done or not, I've got to come down, because at 7:30 the boat is due to arrive."

The early morning photo was scheduled for two weeks later. But following this interview Eddy Adams,a Pulitzer Prize winning photographer, came to take his shots from the ground.

Charlie told one of the rangers, "I've got to go up on the Flame and check a few things out. So if you see me up there, don't worry about it." They trusted him.

The photographer set up his tripod down below and shot several photos of Charlie atop the Flame. When it was over, the photographer's assistant told Charlie, "When I saw you climb off the golden Flame, without the aid of a ladder, I almost freaked out!"

Totally without fear of heights, Charlie answered, "You get used to it. It's no big thing."

Two days later, Charlie got a call from Timothy White, the photographer that *PARADE* had asked to take the photo from a helicopter. After Charlie explained his plan, the photographer agreed to it and said he would be in touch with the pilot.

The next day Mr. White called, reporting that the pilot said he had to stay 1,500 feet away from the Statue.

"Timothy, that's not so," said Charlie. "That way I'd be a tiny speck in the picture!'

"Yes, I know. It's too great a distance!"

"Timothy, I know FAA rules. Your helicopter pilot can come within 200 feet of the Statue of Liberty. Copters are always coming close to the Torch."

"Yes, but he's scared he's going to have his license suspended."

"I'll tell you what I'll do. I'll pray about this, and if God wants this shot, it's going to be done. God will get it done!"

Timothy called the next day, saying the pilot agreed

to fly, but didn't know how close he could come to the Flame.

The big moment came. Charlie stayed overnight on the third floor of the pedestal in a storeroom where he kept his climbing gear, backpack vacuum, safety harness, ropes and light bulbs for his work at the Statue.

Charlie prayed, *"Dear Lord, the desire for me to do this is still strong. I take it that Your Holy Spirit is telling me this is what You want, to be glorified by it. Please make everything go right. It is in Your hands."*

Unable to sleep a wink, he kept walking outside on the promenade and checking the weather. At 5 o'clock in the morning his excitement began to build, and his heart was pounding!

At 5:30 he began the 30-story climb up the stairs to the Torch, arriving there about 5:45. Physically pulling his body up from the catwalk in one motion, he grabbed the lower points of the golden Flame and jumped on top, without the aid of a ladder, at 6:05!

"It was a beautiful morning, with hardly any wind, which was really a blessing. I've been up there when the winds have exceeded 80 and 90 miles an hour. With even a 40 or 50-mile an hour wind, the Torch and Flame begin to sway six inches!

"As I looked up at the sky, the sun was starting to rise in the east, about even with the Brooklyn Bridge. It was a beautiful sight, and I breathed a prayer, *'Dear Lord, just this one time in my life!'*

"I heard the noise of the helicopter coming down the Hudson! I said, 'Dear Lord, is it Timothy?' I was really excited!

"Sure enough, when the helicopter got close, it made a right turn, and I could see Timothy White hanging out the door of the cockpit!! I learned later he had two assistants with him, loading film for him, color and black and white.

"I began to pose. The first pose was of me waving the flag. To my delight the pilot came within 60 or 70 feet of the Torch. Sometimes he came as close as 35 or 40 feet! It was awesome!!"

Charlie went all out for the full 30-minute photo shoot, waving the flag from every conceivable position — standing up, squatting down. With a wet rag, he simulated washing the seagull droppings from the top of the golden Flame, then stood up with his hands on his hips!

"Finally, at 6:45, I waved to Timothy and started the climb down off the Flame onto the catwalk. The helicopter made a wide turn, heading toward the Hudson River, back to its heliport in New Jersey. I knew it was a wrap. We did it!

"Without God it never could have happened! He came through in a tremendous way. I saw His power and His hand in it all!

"On Sunday, July 1st, 1990, I ran down to the newsstand, grabbed a copy of the *New York Daily News*, looking for the *PARADE* magazine insert. Sure enough, there I was on the front cover, standing on top of the golden Flame!

"I bought ten copies. The guy at the newsstand looked at me and said, 'You must like this newspaper!' I said, 'I'm in it! I'm in it!'"

Charlie went from newsstand to newsstand, gathering more than 40 *PARADE* magazine inserts, throwing away the rest of the *New York Daily News*. The people at *PARADE* also called, saying they had set aside 60 copies for him.

"Because of my actions in not getting permission from Superintendent Kevin Buckley, I received a letter from him. I understood why. I had put him, as well as Deputy Superintendent Tom Bradley and the Park Service, in a difficult position.

"On my part, I felt very strongly that this was God's will, that He would be glorified by this photo and the story that ran with it which also mentioned the Lord's name.

"When I first climbed on top of the golden Flame in 1989 to clean off the seagull droppings, that's when I discovered the very tip of the golden Flame had several burn marks caused by lightning.

"Later, in December, 1994, I was asked by the Museum curator to climb up on the Flame again to take pictures of those burn marks as I had done in 1989. I found many more burn marks on the tip of the Flame and on other areas on the dome, the lower part of the Flame.

"I shot several rolls of film for the Museum staff which clearly showed the many burn marks on the tip and lower areas of the Flame. If, in 1989, I had not climbed on top of the Flame to clean off the seagull droppings, I would never have seen the burnt marks on the tip of the Flame and lower dome which cannot be seen from the Torch's catwalk below. I had also walked on top of the original copper and glass Flame as well, doing repair work over the years.

"I felt, if I was willing to risk my safety to work on top of the two Flames over the years, I deserved and earned the right to have my photo taken on top of the Flame as well.

"For the next couple of weeks, whenever I saw Mr. Buckley, I'd shy away from him, thinking he would chew me out. But he was a gentleman. He never said anything.

He had to do what he had to do."

Because of the *PARADE* magazine article, mail began pouring in, including a letter of commendation from President George Bush "citing Charles DeLeo for his dedication as 'Keeper of the Flame' and hard work, a lover of America."

Reader's Digest ran the story in condensed form along with the photo of Charlie standing atop the Flame. *Guideposts* also ran a short feature.

"Then I got a call from Mark Goodson Productions in Los Angeles. They were redoing the show, 'To Tell The Truth', and wanted me to be a guest on the TV program. When I was a kid, growing up in the 50's, my Mom used to love that show, and so did I.

"One of the things I wanted to do as a guest on that program was to glorify God in some way.

"They were taping 14 shows in that one day. One of the cast members was Kitty Carlisle, a gracious celebrity, along with Morton Downey and others. My segment was next to the last so I spent the whole day getting ready.

"I had to bring three of my Park Service uniforms, one for me and one each for the two 'impostors' who would claim to be me on the show. One was an actor and the other was a fellow who worked for a pharmaceutical company.

"I sat in the middle between them. Three out of the four panel members guessed it was me. Only one said, 'It could be #2, but probably not.' My evident enthusiasm made me a dead giveaway.

"At the end of the segment, the emcee said, 'Will the real Charlie DeLeo please stand up.' Everybody applauded as I stood. The emcee asked me about my position at the Statue, and I said, '*I really believe God saved my life in Vietnam and predestinated me to be the Keeper of the Flame of that magnificent Lady!'*

"The panelists were in tears. Then the emcee said, 'Charlie, you wrote a poem about the Statue in the words of Lady Liberty. Could you recite it for us?'

"I said:

*Great God has placed me where I am
and fashioned me with wondrous care.*

*He always hears my silent prayers.
I have a soul.*

I care, I care.

"Isn't it amazing how God gave me that opportunity at just the right moment, to glorify Him? The Holy Spirit just alerted me and I did it! I did it!

TWENTY TWO

Nevada's Mystery

Charlie was excited about what God had done for him. He'd take the cover of *PARADE* showing him atop the golden Flame and lift it above his head and praise the Lord! He was on cloud 9!

One day he took it with him on a visit to the Lower East Side. He sat on the stoop of the tenement house at 104 Forsythe Street where he was born and grew up, re-reading the article about him in *PARADE*.

Memories of the good times with Miss Briggs welled up inside him as he strolled through Roosevelt Park. Holding his magazine cover close to his heart, he began to pray.

"Thank You, Heavenly Father, for the way You have protected and guided me all these years, beginning in this neighborhood, sparing my life in Vietnam, and now allowing the story of how You have blessed my life to be known throughout the world.

"Without You, this could never have happened. I give You all the honor and the glory and the praise!"

Everywhere Charlie went, especially up in the Torch, he'd hold the magazine cover high and saturate his prayer chapel with praise!

But, along with these blessings, came another trying time for Charlie. In January 1991 he noticed his beloved little cat, Chico, was not eating right and was thin as a rail. He drooled at the mouth, the drool giving off a foul odor.

"I knew Chico was about to die. I thanked God for giving me the privilege of having him as my little companion for 16 years.

"There was a place on Ellis Island where I would often pray. I dug a grave there for Chico, knowing I would soon take him to the vet and have him put to sleep.

"That weekend was a rough one. Chico didn't eat a thing. He sat in my lap and looked at me like he was trying to say, *'It's okay, Charlie, my time is up, and your time is still here. Don't worry about it.'*

"Monday morning I woke up and called a cab. I took Chico in a cat box to the vet. 'He is 16 years old,' I told the lady, 'and he seems so thin.'

She said, "He's very dehydrated."

"I asked, 'Does he have a disease?'

She said, "It could be cancer. The best thing to do is to put him to sleep. At his age, there's very little hope. He is suffering. Would you like to wait in the other room while I put him to sleep?"

"No, I want to be here till the last with Chico."

"Well, you could hold him down," she said.

"Chico looked at me, and I took his weak little 'meow' as him saying, 'Goodbye, Charlie.'

"With me and the assistant holding Chico, the lady vet gave him one shot, and he was still living; then a second shot, and his eyes closed. He was gone."

"On Monday, I took the early 6:30 a.m. boat to work because I wanted to bury Chico, and still be able to make it to the Statue by 7:30 to begin work.

"I had wrapped his body in a new white sheet and placed him in a duffle bag that I bought for his burial. Then, very gently I laid him in the litttle grave and covered him.

"Each evening when I came home from work, Chico had always been by the door, waiting for me. The first thing I did was to feed him. But, that evening, there was no Chico to meet me.

"I broke down and cried for three hours, like I cried when I lost my mother. And the next day I came home and cried for two hours.

"But after that I started to get better. As I carried my Mom always in my heart, so I carried Chico in my heart. God couldn't have given me a more wonderful pet."

In 1992 Charlie was called into the office of Assistant Superintendent Larry Steeler, who told him, "We're going to contract the cleaning work you're doing out on the girders. They'll be doing the cleaning in the lobby, the rest rooms, and the spiral stairs.

"But we're going to offer an option for them to clean the iron girders. How do you feel about that?"

"Well, Larry, I've been here for 20 years now, and I've done an awful lot of climbing and work out there. I think my body can no longer continue to take on such a grueling work assignment.'"

He said, "Charlie, all the lights will be yours, including the Torch and Crown lights. You'll still go out on the girders to check the fluorescent lighting.

"It's just the cleaning we're going to offer them. If

they accept, would you be willing to show these contractors your routine of cleaning the Statue interior?"

"Yes, sir, I'd be pleased to do that."

Charlie took five contractors to the base of the spiral staircase where, looking up, they could see the entire 70,000 cubic feet of the iron skeleton, copper shelling snd pylon. One look, and three of the men said they wanted no part of that!

Two of them made their bids, and the contract was awarded to Lower and Company.

"The boss at Lower asked me if I wanted to work for him full-time on the girders. He would pay me double what I was making. That was tempting but I didn't want to give up 20 years of working at the Statue. Also, I had time in the military that would be credited toward retirement."

Charlie took a couple of the workers and showed them a few moves on the girders, how to do the vacuuming and the washing of the girders, moving from the top on down.

"I myself kept active, checking the light fixtures and structurally inspecting the Statue as best I could. When I ran across loose metal bolts on top of the armature bars I'd retrieve them. They were seven-inch bolts and if they ever fell down, there would be nothing to protect visitors below from getting hit.

"I missed not doing the cleaning, but it had become too hard a task those later years. I had done it for seven years all by myself. At night I often had trouble sleeping due to the sharp pains in my legs.

"I remember one time when I was unhooked from my safety belt and had to jump from the iron skeleton onto one of the copper interior folds of the Lady's drapery.

It was about a four-foot jump, and normally to make that jump would be a piece of cake.

"This time I was short about a foot. I started down what would have been a 60-foot fall! God must have had my guardian angel really grab me fast. After a few feet, I grabbed hold of a stainless steel armature bar and ended up with my left wrist cut, but I was okay.

"There were a lot of experiences like that. People would ask me, 'Would you do this all over again if you could?'

"I said, 'Absolutely. It was God who called me to be the Keeper of the Flame at the Statue of Liberty. He gave me the great honor of being the longest Keeper of the Flame in Lady Liberty's history. I felt, too, that I was a main caretaker of the world's greatest monument to Freedom!

"I felt a special kinship with Quasimodo, the fictional caretaker of Notre Dame Cathedral, as well as with the lighthouse keepers around the world."

Visitors were attracted to Charlie. Many had seen him on the TV shows or read about him in their newspaper. He became like a folk hero, or a Forrest Gump-type figure, whose faith and love were genuine. In every task he took on, he gave it his all, and people loved him for that spirit of giving.

Charlie had his favorites, too.

"In the early 1990's I met a lady, Vera Kleen, and her husband from California here at Liberty Island. We began corresponding and she became very special to me. She sent me cookies now and then.

"Vera was a Seventh Day Adventist who really lived the Bible and the Gospel, and the Sermon on the Mount. She loved God and His Son Jesus, her Savior.

"Her husband died a few years ago. But she remained actively involved in charities and church work. To me she has been a real inspiration!

"I think of Gabe Madison, one of our boat captains for 16 years at the Statue of Liberty. He ran both the Liberty II and the Liberty III. He retired some years back, and now lives in South Carolina.

On several occasions I had the privilege of dating his beautiful daughter, Maria Madison. She was a lovely young woman, and a very dedicated worker, like her Dad.

"A couple of years ago, Gabe came for a visit. He had never been up to the Torch. So I got to take him up there. At first, he seemed nervous, but he made it.

"Of all the people with whom I have ever worked, no one has believed in me more over my 30 years as Liberty's Keeper or has been more supportive of me and my work, than Ranger Doug Treem, an eight-year veteran at the Statue, whom I have taken up to the Torch twice.

"Born in Nebraska in 1950, now living in Manhattan, Doug is truly a remarkable and giving person, a real people person, the best Ranger I have ever known at the Statue of Liberty.

"Wise and gentle, loving and caring, he is a very deeply spiritual man who truly loves God and his fellow-man. He treats every visitor as being very special, and is an expert on the Statue's history. We have done hundreds of Statue tours with the visitors over the years.

"I do Statue tours with other Rangers, but I really love and look forward to Doug's tour more than any other Statue tour. We are a great team together, and the National Park Service should be proud to know that Ranger Doug Treem represents the Service in the highest and most outstanding way.

"Doug has been a great help and comfort to me over the years and, at the drop of a hat, would give me the shirt off his back if I asked him.

"Like me, Doug is a poet. He is also an actor and playwright who has starred in some off Broadway plays which he has written.

"He is a truly remarkable man and a credit to America, the National Park Service, and to Lady Liberty and all that she stands for. I salute you, Doug Treem, and may God always bless you, dear friend.

"In 1998 Becky Brock, an outstanding ranger at the Statue, introduced me to her girl friend, Nevada Barr, and asked if I would take them on a tour of the Torch.

"In our conversation I learned Nevada would be staying with Becky for a couple of weeks, doing research on a book about the Statue of Liberty. And it was to be a murder mystery!

"She said, 'Charlie, you seem to be an interesting person. Can you tell me more about yourself and your job here at the Statue?' I was always glad to do that!

"She listened without taking any notes and then asked me, 'Can I use you as a character in one of the books?'

"I said, 'O, yeah, I'd be proud. By all means!' " She said, 'Okay.'"

They parted, and Charlie forgot about their meeting. A year later, one of the rangers, Elizabeth Carroll, said to Charlie, "I just read about you in a book."

"I said, 'What are you talking about — a book?'

She said, "Yes, it's called, 'Liberty Falling' by Nevada Barr."

"O, yes," I said. "That's the lady. I remember her."

"I went to Barnes and Noble and browsed through

the book to find where she was referring to me as Keeper of the Flame at the Statue of Liberty. She described how I felt about Lady Liberty and my climbing skills. She was very flattering in describing me.

"Near the end she described her being up in the Torch. 'I felt the hush of Charlie's chapel and the nearness of Charlie's God.' In another chapter she wrote, 'The Torch was like a chapel, so high, close to God, with a humbling view of His world.'

"Imagine that! In that secular mystery book, the plot of which was the destruction of the Statue, a book which was on the *New York Times* 'Best Seller' list, Nevada Barr describes in great detail my love for God and for Lady Liberty!

TWENTY THREE

Through It All

Charlie was on his way to the Statue one day when a visitor stopped him, "Excuse me, sir. Do you work here? There's a big goose stuck in a tree. He's upside down and wedged and can't get free."

"Sure enough, it was one of the Canadian geese that frequent Liberty Island. It had crashed into a tree and one foot was wedged tight between two branches.

"He was 25 feet up in the tree, so I got a ladder and climbed as high as I could go. To get him free I managed to break loose one of the branches that held him captive. He fell to the ground and flew away.

"In the past I had rescued a number of pigeons and sparrows stuck in the old glass and copper Flame, and sparrows gathered inside the Crown who couldn't get free.

"I felt good being able to do that. I love animals. God put them here to make man's life more pleasant in this world, and for us to be stewards, taking care of these creatures that He created."

Speaking of feeling good, March 22, 1997 was

Charlie's 25th anniversary as Keeper of the Flame at the Statue of Liberty. A group of rangers arranged a party for him, and Superintendent Diane Dayson granted permission for members of the staffs from Liberty Island and Ellis Island to take off work and attend it.

"To my surprise, my old coworkers showed up — 'Big Mike' Cantanowicz who started work as boat captain in 1976. He brought with him Jimmy Benton, my Vietnam veteran buddy and mentor who trained me on the girders.

"A lot of the rangers were there, including Dave McCutcheon, and Doug Treem who gave me a wonderful tribute, along with many of the U.S. Park Police.

"Sylvia Sanchez, the First Lady of the Island, was there. She began work at the Statue of Liberty's gift shop back in 1954, and had been such an inspiration to me. We'd talk about the Lord every time we'd meet.

"The same is true of Nilda Inlan, a hard worker for the past 20 years at the Statue, who helped me clean the girders.

'Ruby Hopkins was there, the best personnel officer I ever saw work at the Statue, and her assistant, Jackie Martinez. What a team they were!"

The event was written up in the *New York Daily News*, a beautiful article by Vick Viegler.

Charlie always hoped that God would make it possible for him to be interviewed by Charles Kerault on his "Sunday Morning" program. But it never came to pass for an in person interview.

Instead, Mr. Kerault found out about Charlie and wanted him to appear in his "American Moments" TV series, and sent a film crew to cover the story.

It worked out well. In it Charlie is climbing the girders and up in the Torch, and Charles Kerault, on a voice over, is talking about him. At the end of the segment, Mr. Kerault appears in a studio shot, saying, 'In our day, the only one to ever keep her light from above is Charlie DeLeo, the Keeper of the Flame.'

Another surprise around that time was a call from CBS Evening News. Harry Smith wanted to do a story on Charlie. The CBS program was not only seen nationwide but all over the world!

Mr. Smith arrived on the morning of the shoot with a film crew. The film shows him talking to Charlie on the boat on the way over to the Statue, about him serving in Vietnam and being awarded the Purple Heart.

In the next scene Charlie is climbing the girders, and Harry says, "With the strength and skill of a gymnast, Charlie inspects the girders that hold Liberty together."

"Superintendent Dayson had me wear a helmet while climbing the ladder to the Torch. Then I was filmed in the crown from a helicopter.

"One of the things I said on the segment was, 'I love going up to the Torch. It is like a chapel to me. I feel close to God up there. And I ask God to bless all people that are searching for liberty's meaning.'

"I was able to glorify God in this CBS Evening News piece that was shown worldwide!"

At the end of the segment, Charlie says to Harry Smith, *"I've seen what war can do. Nobody wins in a war. But the only thing worse than war is slavery. And as long as Lady Liberty is standing on her pedestal, we're free!"*

Harry Smith says, "And as long as Charlie is keeping the Flame, Liberty's light will always shine!"

"It was a great piece! Harry Smith was great to work with, a down to earth guy.

"For my 25th Anniversary in March, 1997 I had

been privileged to be filmed by a film crew from Charles Kerault for 'American Moments', and 'CBS Evening News' with Harry Smith.

"July 4, 1997 was a sad day.   We learned that Charles Kerault had died. I figured, when CBS Evening News began to broadcast a tribute to him, that my segment would be postponed because he was such a great man. It would probably be all about him. "But I admired him and figured I'd watch the whole news about his passing."

Towards the last part of the segment, I was surprised when the newscaster started to present my story. Sure enough, my segment with Harry Smith ran in its entirety. He did a great job of editing it to fit it in.

"Shortly after that, Harry Smith called me and I told him about that. I said, 'Harry, I thought my piece would not be aired on that particular Friday evening.'

"He said, 'We decided to run your segment with the tribute to Charles Kerault, because your story is a Charles Kerault story!' "

In 1998, a colleague of Charles Kerault published a book by Simon and Shuster, "American Moments with Charles Kerault".   It included a couple of pages about Charlie, and the story about him that was featured in the film, 'American Moments'.

Things were going good for Charlie in one area of his life. His story was known throughout the world. But, in his body, he was feeling a lot of aches and pains. His years of climbing the girders and lifting heavy loads up and down the inner superstructure of the Statue were beginning to take their toll on him.

There was no question about his love for Lady Liberty and his devotion to his work. God had done great and miraculous things with his life for 27 and a half years as "Keeper of the Flame", and while making his 2,500 climbs to the Torch as self-appointed caretaker!

After talking to Ruby Hopkins in personnel about early retirement, including his credit for four years in the military, he decided to make the move.

"My last day was October 1, 1999. They threw a retirement party for me.

"But, when I got home, I felt absolutely unprepared for retirement. I just couldn't believe that I had given up one of the world's most unique and interesting jobs where God was still doing interesting and mighty things with my life.

"I was the senior staff member for the entire National Park Service represented at the Statue of Liberty. God had made me well known and famous all over the world.

"On the spur of the moment, I had signed it all away!

"I went into a state of shock. At times I would get up in the middle of the night. I thought I was suffocating! I was now a civilian — retired!!

After months in agony, Charlie called Frank Mills, Assistant Superintendent at the Statue. He arranged for him to come back as a volunteer, to do maintenance work and assigments that were not hazardous .

"But after three months of volunteering, I again felt the urge to leave. I was going through some rough times!

"But then, on August 20, 2000, I went to my holy of holies, Cypress Hills National Cemetery, in need of God's comfort and love. The Holy Spirit moved upon me during four and a half hours of prayer and praise, and I came out of there, refreshed, confident and strong again!

"It wasn't until a few months later, on December 4, 2000 that I came back to the Statue of Liberty as a volunteer.

"I had said, 'Lord, do something so great with my life that I'll know that You are still with me."   I had thought I had betrayed the Lord, because I had not consulted with Him at all, and He had allowed me to go through this rough period.

"The Bible says, 'Whom the Lord loveth, He chastens.'

"Again I talked to Frank Mills. He said, 'Come on, Charlie. We want you back!'

"So I came back again, and the Holy Spirit moved me to start making copies of my *Reader's Digest* story, my poem, "This Lady Prays", and my retirement story in the *New York Daily News*, to pass them out to the visitors.

"I laminated the picture of me in *PARADE* magazine, showing me standing on top of the Flame waving a flag. As I told my story, the visitors, especially school teachers, were so impressed. They wanted to know more.

"Since then, I have literally shared my story in person and given out thousands of copies of my story in *Reader's Digest* and my poem, 'This Lady Prays'

"God is doing great things in my life. In less than a year, I reached more people on a one-to-one basis than I ever reached personally in my 27 and a half years as the active Keeper of the Flame at the Statue

"Of course, through the media throughout my entire career, I reached millions of people all over the world. At least a dozen foreign magazines featured me, including the November, 1998 issue of *Der Spiegel*, the TIME magazine of Germany, one of the foremost publications in all of Europe.

"I was really proud of the article about me in the November, 1998 issue of the Marine Corps publication, *Leatherneck* magazine. Lieutenant Colonel Leonard Sheldon and his wife visited me at the Statue of Liberty.

"The best story ever written about me was the *Los Angeles Times* article by Dave Smith in April, 1979. But this one in the Marine Corps magazine was the most patriotic story of all.

"Lieutenant Colonel Sheldon did a superb job in capturing the way I really believed in the Statue of Liberty. He caught my passion and spirit!

"Let's face it, I was a nobody from the Lower East Side, never finished school, tried my best to serve on the front lines in Vietnam, almost got myself killed.

"But I followed my dream of one day climbing the Torch at the Statue of Liberty. From there, the rest is history.

"I never had a press agent or a PR man. If I had, he never would have been able to introduce this uneducated, unknown kid to the secular market. A guy who placed his faith in God above all! They would have laughed at me!

"There is only one answer to this riddle called life. It is God through His Son Jesus Christ, indwelling a person through His Holy Spirit!

"The Apostle Paul said, 'It is not I, but Christ liveth in me. I can do all things through Christ who strengtheneth me.'

"And though I wavered at times and left God out of the picture, His promise was still true, '*I will never leave you nor forsake you. I love you with an undying love.*'

"*The Lord is not only a Lover, He is a Savior, a Giver and a Healer!*

After 20 months of laying off climbing the girders,

Charlie wanted to see if he could still do it. At age 53, he climbed to the top of the Torch, from girder to girder, as good as when he was in his prime!

God is good!

TWENTY FOUR

The New Millennium

The Twentieth Century ended December 31, 2000. The Twenty First Century, or New Millennium, began one minute after midnight, on January 1, 2001.

To celebrate that historic date, Charlie wanted to go up in the Torch but he did not have access to the keys. Jeff Marrazzo, the new caretaker, assured him he would arrange for Charlie to be the first one up in the Torch on January 2nd of the new century.

"In the meantime, I made sure I'd be the first one at Cypress Hills National Cemetery on January 1, 2001 to begin the New Millennium in prayer in that sacred place.

"The day before we had had a big snowstorm with two feet of snow. Normally the cemetery opened at eight o' clock but that day the main gate was closed. I found a little side gate that was open.

"I was determined to be the first man up on that hill. Some of the snowdrifts were three feet high. It took a lot of physical exertion for me to get from the bottom of the Cemetery the 400 or 500 yards to where the roadway winds around to the top of the hill.

"I had to stop several times. But I made it up there. The best part was there were no tire marks or footprints, so I knew no one had been up there since the snowstorm!

"I had always said that I would like to be alive when God sends His Son back into the world to take His people Home. And that I would like to be up on that holy hill of all the places in the world, my 'holy of holies'!

"What a privilege God had given me — those thousands of trips up there for the past 32 years! This one meant so much to me. The fresh new blanket of snow covering that hillside was a beautiful sight. I was reminded of God's promise to all believers, 'Though your sins be as scarlet, they shall be white as snow!'

"I prayed and recommitted my life to God and to Christ my Savior."

The next morning, January 2, 2001, as a volunteer, Charlie boarded the National Park Service staff boat for Liberty Island. Jeff met him with a smile and a cheery greeting, "Good morning, Charlie, are you ready to go? I have just a little paper work to finish and I'll be right with you."

"What if I meet you up in the crown," I said, "and then we can go from there to the Torch?" He said, "Fine!"

The elevator was on the sixth floor, so Charlie decided to climb the pedestal and on up the spiral staircase to the crown, as he had done for all those years.

Waiting up there for Jeff, he prayed, "Lord, I would really like to change the first burned out light bulb in the Torch in the New Millennium. That would mean I'd be the only human being to do that in two continuous centuries!"

Jeff soon showed up at the door leading to the

climb to the Torch, handed Charlie the key, assuring him, "Charlie, here's the key. You are the first one in the new Millennium to open the door to the Torch. You lead the way!"

Holding a bucket of light bulbs in one hand, and the tools to change the lights in the other hand, Charlie led the way up the 42-foot ladder inside the Lady's right arm to the Torch. He prayed as he made what he considered a historic move in his life, "Lord, let there be at least one burned out light bulb!"

"Jeff was a man of his word. He let me climb the ladder before him up to the Torch. Sure enough, when we opened the door to the catwalk surrounding the Torch, there were two burned out light bulbs!

"I had bought a disposable camera which I handed to Jeff. He was kind enough to take pictures of me changing the first burned out light bulbs at the Torch in the New Millennium.

"He also took pictures of me holding the PARADE magazine cover, showing me standing atop the golden Flame and waving a flag!

"Jeff was a first class act. Since I had been volunteering for the three months in the year 2000 and now beginning the New Millennium, he had allowed me to make 14 climbs to the Torch, where I had changed 30 burned out light bulbs. I am the only volunteer ever privileged to do that!

"Incidentally, the most light bulbs I ever changed at one time in the Torch was eight. On two occasions, I changed eight. Both times were in the winter, with a wind chill of minus 10 or 20 degrees below zero! That wind just tore me up. It froze my fingers. I had fought the bitter cold up there for many, many years.

"Here I am, 53, retired and serving as a volunteer. I know that isn't very old, but if you have had the kind of physical abuse on your body that I have had, you'd think differently. Yet I find I still have the spring in my legs and ankles, and I haven't lost my climbing skills!

"I just want to salute all the men and women in charge of the Statue under whom I worked over the years — the superintendents, chiefs of maintenance, my supervisors and co-workers.

"There were times when some of my superiors just didn't understand all the media exposure that the Lord was giving me. Many were gracious about it, but still didn't understand.

"But, overall, they were very supportive of me. I could understand their situation. They were in charge of the Statue of Liberty, our national monument. And there I was, often in demand by the media, whether television, newspapers, magazines or radio.

"This was my calling from God, and I had to bear a cross. There were times when it wasn't easy to bear that cross, when I didn't have the Christian courage, or I didn't practice what I preached.

"But, you know, a Christian is to walk by faith and not by sight. Our climb is to be an upward march, a global pilgrimage.

"In all my trials and tribulations, Christ was always by my side. At times, when I was too exhausted to go on, He carried me over the rough terrain, the jagged rocks and up the hills.

"I owe it all to the mercy and grace of God, and Jesus my Savior."

TWENTY FIVE

A Day of Infamy

Tuesday, September 11, 2001— Charlie DeLeo was making his morning rounds of Lady Liberty, from the top of her Torch to her unshackled feet.

At 8:20 a.m., checking the lights at the observation balcony, he turned to take in the breathtaking view of the focal point of lower Manhattan, the World Trade Center with its majestic Twin Towers, bathed in the sunlight of a beautiful September morn! The Big Apple at its best!

In one hour the first boatload of tourists would dock at Liberty Island. At 8:42 a.m. Charlie rode the elevator down to the ground level of the pedestal, the base of the Statue.

"Once outside, my eyes turned again to the Twin Towers," said Charlie. "I could hardly believe my eyes! I saw a massive inferno raging on the top floors of Tower #1! At first, I thought some steam pipes might have burst. And then I thought probably a bomb — but from that high up? It looked really bad!"

Charlie immediately began praying for God's protection over the people trapped in those upper floors of Tower #1.

"At 8:55 a.m., I suddenly heard the roar of jet engines overhead!" Charlie recalled. "I looked up, to see a giant airliner, less than 200 feet above the Flame held high by Lady Liberty. It was heading on a direct course toward Tower #2!"

9:02 a.m., United Airlines Flight 175 slammed into the south Tower of the World Trade Center. In utter disbelief, a nation and a world suddenly woke up to the horrifying reality that nothing it had witnessed that morning had been accidental.

It was a national tragedy, a holocaust of hate at America's doorstep!

Maintenance and office workers at the Statue, upon hearing the news, hurried down to the sea wall to get a better look at what was happening. They fumbled for coins to activate the binoculars placed there for tourists to get a close-up of Manhattan.

"At that moment I could hear some of our workers screaming and cursing at whoever was behind this horrendous attack."

A U.S. police officer reported he could see a man jumping to his death from the top floor of Tower #1. The group gasped in horror at the thought!

Charlie began praying for the Statue to be spared the same tragic fate as the Towers.

Fifteen minutes later the U.S. Park police ordered everybody off Liberty Island and onto boats, some heading for nearby Ellis Island and the rest for Manhattan.

"Sitting in the bow of the boat, I was aghast, staring at both Twin Towers aflame. It was like watching some 'End of the World' disaster movie. I thought of those poor people trapped inside the Towers.

"As we drew closer to Manhattan, I saw the fire on both Towers more clearly. It was like the worst nightmare one could ever dream!"

The boat docked at the Coast Guard pier next to the Staten Island ferry terminal. Gathered outside were thousands of people, frantically seeking a way out of this hell on earth, anxious to be evacuated.

Soon a massive wave of media reports began to span the globe: "Four passenger jets departed within 42 minutes of one another from three East Coast airports. The planes were transformed by hijackers into fuel-laden missiles. Two pierced the Twin Towers in New York City, causing massive damage. Another rammed into the Pentagon building in Washington, D.C. The fourth crashed in a field outside Pittsburgh, reported to have originally been headed for the Capitol in D.C."

"I stood at the end of the pier, looking at Lady Liberty for a couple of minutes. Then my eyes turned in the direction of the Twin Towers ten short blocks to the north.

"From that point, I couldn't see the Trade Towers. Nearby tall buildings blocked the view. But I could see massive billows of smoke and smell acid fumes coming from this colossal conflagration!

"A couple of men joined me on the pier. Before we knew it, there were 10 or 12 of us. Many agreed, 'If another plane hits the Towers, they will crumble. All that thick smoke could choke us.'

"Fearing smoke inhalation, a young man scurried down the ladder to the river's edge, carrying our tee shirts to soak in the water. In case of emergency, the wet garment, held to our nose, would help protect us from the deadly smoke.

"All of a sudden, we heard a loud explosion. Unable to see the Towers from that vantage point, we stood in awe as the sky was filled with showering fragments of steel, aluminum and glass flying everywhere. The noise was deafening. We were told it was the result of Tower #2 coming down — all 110 stories reduced to tons of rubble—in an instant!!

"Bits of flying debris reached the area around the pier. We heard radio reports of pandemonium at the site of the World Trade Center — zombie-looking survivors running for their lives, their faces and business attire covered with a clay-like mixture of dust and ashes from the building and offices that minutes before were the source of their livelihood!

"Twenty minutes later, Tower #1 crashed down, reduced to a wasteland, soon to be called 'Ground Zero'. As oily smoke blocked out September's morning sun, the wet tee shirts helped shield us from its deadly peril."

For some, the black oily smoke was a grim reminder of the attack on Pearl Harbor, named "A Day of Infamy" by President Roosevelt.

Soon the U.S. Park police boat arrived. The police began evacuating the group on the pier. Charlie alone waived their offer, thinking, *"I've got to stand by Lady Liberty, focusing my prayers on her, and on the victims of this horrible tragedy."*

For an hour and a half, Charlie helped secure police and fire boats and small craft as they tied up at the dock.

"Then I saw a sight I'd never seen before in my almost 30 years of working at the Statue in the New York harbor. I watched tugboats from a variety of tugboat companies pull up alongside to rescue victims of the disaster and whisk them away to safety. It was really inspiring to see New York at its most tragic, and yet, its finest, hour!"

Charlie's desire as Keeper of the Flame at the Statue, was to be close to Lady Liberty on Liberty Island, but the U.S. Park police had it blocked off. After three hours of helping where he could at the pier, he walked to nearby Battery Park where he hailed a tugboat loaded with close to 100 needy passengers. He was ready to head home.

"They picked me up and, as we moved north up the East River, we were faced with a ghastly, heart-wrenching, sight—Manhattan's skyline minus the Twin Trade Towers. Unbelievable!!"

Each passenger looked on in numbed silence, many with hot tears flooding their vision. But, as is often said, truth is stranger than fiction. It took several years to erect this architectural wonder, but less than an hour and a half to completely demolish it!

On the long way home to Brooklyn via tugboat, bus and finally the subway, Charlie's mind filled with many bittersweet memories of earlier days in this neighborhood:

"When I first started working at the Statue of Liberty in March, 1972, every time I climbed the ladder to Lady Liberty's torch, I was fascinated by the view of the World Trade Center Towers under construction.

"I marvelled at the engineering skill and the three sets of workers toiling 24 hours a day every day building this amazingly unique set of twin skyscrapers.

"I remember when Tower #2 reached its final height of 110 stories and they topped it off with a big flag. Months later, I watched Tower #1's construction completed, with a 210-foot antenna added.

"I could hardly wait for opening day when I could ride the elevator to the observation desk on Tower #2 and take in the incredible view of New York harbor and Liberty Island. There was Lady Liberty, standing proudly on her pedestal and majestically holding her Torch in her strong right arm, the tip of her Flame pointing to Heaven itself, as if pointing to God, the true Source of Life and Liberty!

"One time I took a young lady on a dinner date to a restaurant on the top floor of Tower #2, called 'Windows on the World.' We were able to look out the windows as we dined and enjoy the view of the Statue of Liberty in the harbor, all lit up — a gorgeous sight!

"I recall, on ten different occasions, donating blood at the World Trade Center in one of the smaller buildings in front of Twin Tower #2, named Building #5 which was only seven stories high."

With only three more stops on the subway before reaching home, Charlie decided to get off at "Cypress Hills" for a time of prayer at his favorite place, the Cypress Hills National Veterans Memorial Cemetery.

Completely exhausted, the 53-year-old Vietnam veteran found a quiet spot on a hill overlooking the graves of fellow veterans, dating back to the Civil War.

There he poured out his heart to the Lord in prayer and praise to the One who had been such a loving Father to him all his life and helped him realize his childhood dream of being the Keeper of the Flame at the Statue of Liberty.

The prayer of his heart was for America in that historic hour, that "her heart will be directed to You, dear Lord, and that Lady Liberty's Torch of Freedom will shine bright for all people everywhere, those 'huddled masses yearning to breathe free', including the families of the thousands of victims of today's grim holocaust of hate."

September 11, 2001 became a day deeply engraved in the memory of all Americans . . . a time when the stars and stripes took on new meaning . . . a time when Lady Liberty stood strong, the symbol of victory over tyranny and terrorism . . .

. . . a time when the faith of this nation's founding fathers could no longer be ignored or denied, but rather renewed across this beloved land!

"My country, tis of Thee, sweet land of liberty!"

TWENTY SIX

"Ground Zero"

"On Monday morning, September 17, 2001, six days after that 'Day of Infamy', I decided to walk from my home in Brooklyn across the Brooklyn Bridge, and try to get near where the Twin Towers had been, an area by then called 'Ground Zero'.

"I got downtown in Manhattan, walked around Wall Street, and then headed toward the site where the Twin Towers had been. But the area was completely blocked off with police barricades, and there were police and fire vehicles everywhere.

"From one point near Wall Street I caught a glimpse of what was left after that 'holocaust of hate'. Still standing, at a macabre angle, was a twisted piece of the aluminum and steel facade of the once magnificent 110-story Tower #1! The area was packed with rescue workers!

"Trying to get a better overview of 'Ground Zero', I returned to the Brooklyn Bridge. As I walked farther along the Bridge, I could see more of the Manhattan skyline.

There was only smoke where once stood the Towers, now gone forever!

"I walked to the first stone towers of the Bridge. A CNN film crew was interviewing people, taping their reactions. I shared with them, 'I witnessed a lot of horror while serving in Vietnam, but that doesn't even come close to what happened here on 9/11 Day.'"

When the crew learned of Charlie's relationship to the Statue, they became interested in doing a live TV interview with him at noon on CNN News. It was close to 11 o'clock, so Charlie agreed to wait around.

Ten minutes later the anchor man was on his cell phone. He was told that officials wanted the news media people off the bridge. That meant no interview.

Charlie continued his walk toward the Brooklyn side of the Bridge, then turned around. With tears welling up in his eyes, he took one last look at the emptiness in the once majestic skyline.

He began to pray, *"Lord, protect the rescuers, the firemen and the police, the EMTs, construction workers, and the National Guard.*

"If there be any victims buried alive under the rubble, God, let them be rescued. And Lord, be with the families of the thousands of victims of this terrible tragedy, the innocent passengers in the airplanes and the office personnel that perished trying to flee this inferno!"

Charlie headed home, arriving at 1:45 p.m. For a few minutes he chatted with his uncle Pat on the front steps of the house they shared on Hemlock Street.

"I began to feel a little nauseated and very weak. All of a sudden, I felt a compression in my chest. My jaw began to ache!

"I knew something was wrong, and remembered

saying to my uncle, 'I'm going upstairs and rest for a few minutes.' As soon as I sat down on my living room couch, I realized I was having a heart attack!

"I called to my uncle, '*Dial 911. I think I'm having a heart attack!*' "

Within minutes, the ambulance arrived. The paramedic, a New York City fireman, placed a nitroglycerin tablet underneath Charlie's tongue as he was wheeled out to the waiting mobile hospital vehicle!

"We were on our way! At first the nitroglycerin helped relieve the pressure in my chest, but then the pain returned. Before we arrived at Jamaica Hospital in Queens, I was given a second tablet."

In the emergency room, a team of doctors and nurses tried every means to stabilize Charlie's heart.

"At that point, the pain was so great, I felt like I was at my own 'ground zero', being crushed to death. For the moment I didn't know if I were going to survive this ordeal!!

"But, through it all, God and the Lord Jesus, my Savior, were on my mind constantly. I knew that, by His grace, I would survive!"

Charlie's heart slowed down. Again, the nitroglycerin helped for a time, but then the pain grew worse. The decision was made to transfer him to Lenox Hill Hospital at 77th Street and Lenox Avenue in Manhattan, one of the world's finest coronary hospitals.

Upon arrival at Lenox Hill Hospital, Xrays were taken, showing his right coronary artery was blocked 100 percent. This had caused the heart attack. It was decided, with Charlie's permission, to implant a stint to open up the clogged artery.

"Before being wheeled into the operating room, I

caught a glimpse of my photo on the night stand, showing me standing atop the Flame — a reminder of God's faithfulness!

"I put my life in the hands of Jesus, The Great Physician. Now and then I cried out in pain because my heart was pumping no blood. The pressure was unbelievable . . . like an elephant sitting on my chest!"

An incision was made in Charlie's groin. Up inside the artery, like putting a snake through a clogged sewer line, a balloon was inflated to open up the clogged artery. The stint was then moved into place and expanded to keep the area open.

"My surgeon, Dr. Collins, cleared out the blockage. What a relief I felt! After a 30-minute operation, the 'elephant' was finally off my chest. I praise the Lord for such wonderful care by that fine team of professionals!"

Charlie recovered so well that the doctor decided to do the same operation on the left artery during that same hospital visit. It had showed a 60 percent blockage.

"In between the two operations I got to know the nurses and doctors. After seeing my *PARADE* picture, they became interested in the story behind it, and they asked me, 'Charlie, can we show this to other nurses?' That made me feel good!' "

The morning of his discharge from the hospital, Charlie received a phone call from Jack Anderson, his journalist friend who had become a father figure to him down through the years.

"Charlie, what's happened? I tried to call you all week but the lines were tied up because of '9/11'. Then, when I couldn't get you at home, I knew something was wrong. Knowing you, I thought you might be involved as a volunteer at Ground Zero!

"I called the Statue of Liberty's number, and they told me you had a heart attack! I finally tracked you down. What a relief to hear your voice! How are you doing?"

"Oh, Jack, the Lord is so good! Hearing you is like manna from Heaven! I had a heart attack after walking across the Brooklyn Bridge to Ground Zero to see what was left of the World Trade Center after '9/11'!

"When I got home the pain hit me and my uncle called 9/11. I was rushed first to Jamaica Hospital in Queens and then to Lenox Hill Hospital in Manhattan.

"I had a stint implanted in two arteries, and I'm feeling relieved, though a little weak. They tell me I ate too many fatty foods all my life!"

Jack replied, "Charlie, I really believe that attack was caused by the shock to your heart when you witnessed the assault on our liberty as a nation. Your whole life has been so dedicated to liberty, that it was just too much for you to bear!

"But you're a champion. You're coming out of this. I believe your best years are ahead!

"A lot of people, of all ages, are at their own Ground Zero these days, rethinking their values in life. They wonder about God and how to find Him, and what happens if they suddenly meet death, like those victims of 9/11 did.

"Charlie, they need to hear your story. They need to hear someone genuine, like you, tell it like it is!"

TWENTY SEVEN

Touching People's Lives

"One of Charlie's favorite declarations is: *"Faith is the bugler that never sounds retreat."*

By God's grace and mercy Charlie survived the heart attack he had on September 17, 2001, just six days after "9/11, A Day of Infamy".

But things have changed at the Statue!

The 168 steps of the spiral staircase, from the pedestal to the crown of Lady Liberty, have been closed to both tourists and staff. Tourists are allowed in the Statue's lobby and can enjoy the breathtaking view of Manhattan, Ellis Island, Brooklyn and New Jersey from the observation balcony located just below the feet of Lady Liberty.

They can enjoy the boat ride to Liberty Island, with its inspiring view of the famous Statue, holding high the Flame of Liberty. After the tour, they can visit the concessions, the gift shop and the eating places, with inside and outside dining.

They have read or heard about this Keeper of the Flame, this Vietnam veteran whose patriotic fervor, and very being, are grounded in the love of God and His Word.

Now in his mid-fifties, Charlie is even more in touch with God's plans for his life. He will soon return to the Statue as a volunteer! He will be providing general maintenance of the 150 foot pedestal upon which Lady Liberty stands.

Whenever the media cover the Statue, they always interview Charlie. After three decades as "Keeper of the Flame" and caretaker of the most famous figure in the world, Charlie knows first-hand every inch of Lady Liberty, inside and out.

Reader, if you are planning to visit the Statue of Liberty, be sure to look for Charlie. You will want to see his photos, and hear his presentation about the Statue, with stories of his personal experiences with many of the thousands of visitors from all over the world — people of all races, all nationalities, all ages and interests.

If you were to ask Charlie, "*What is the most important thing in your life?*", he would say, "Being a giver, and knowing God's plan for my life."

Then he would add, "With God's help, I want to touch as many lives as I can in my lifetime."

And Charlie is doing just that, through his service at the Statue, through the 2002 documentary film entitled, "Charlie DeLeo, Keeper of the Flame", and, hopefully, through the reading of this book.

It's easy to understand how Charlie's love affair with Lady Liberty was, and still is, the heart of God's plan for his life.

Printed in the United States
214462BV00001B/5/A

9 781597 819299